# Uncle Tom's Cabin

George Aiken

# THE CAST:

Uncle Tom

George Harris

George Shelby

St. Clare

Phineas Fletcher

Gumption Cute

Mr. Wilson

Deacon Perry

Shelby

Haley

Legree

Tom Loker

Marks

Sambo

Quimbo

Doctor

Waiter

Harry, a child

Eva

Eliza

Cassy

Marie

Ophelia

Chloe

Topsy

## ACT I

## SCENE I

[Plain Chamber. Enter Eliza, meeting George. ]

ELIZA:

Ah! George, is it you? Well, I am so glad you've come. [(George regards her mournfully. )] Why don't you smile, and ask after Harry?

GEORGE:

[(Bitterly. )] I wish he'd never been born! I wish I'd never been born myself!

ELIZA:

[(Sinking her head upon his breast and weeping. )] Oh George!

GEORGE:

There now, Eliza, it's too bad for me to make you feel so. Oh! how I wish you had never seen me — you might have been happy!

ELIZA:

George! George! how can you talk so? What dreadful thing has happened, or is going to happen? I'm sure we've been very happy till lately.

GEORGE:

So we have, dear. But oh! I wish I'd never seen you, nor you me.

ELIZA:

Oh, George! how can you?

GEORGE:

Yes, Eliza, it's all misery! misery! The very life is burning out of me! I'm a poor, miserable, forlorn drudge! I shall only drag you down with me, that's all! What's the use of our trying to do anything — trying to know anything — trying to be anything? I wish I was dead!

ELIZA:

Oh! now, dear George, that is really wicked. I know how you feel about losing your place in the factory, and you have a hard master; but pray be patient —

GEORGE:

Patient! Haven't I been patient? Did I say a word when he came and took me away — for no earthly reason — from the place where everybody was kind to me? I'd paid him truly every cent of my earnings, and they all say I worked well.

ELIZA:

Well, it is dreadful; but, after all, he is your master, you know.

GEORGE:

My master! And who made him my master? That's what I think of. What right has he to me? I'm as much a man as he is. What right has he to make a dray-horse of me? — to take me from things I can do better than he can, and put me to work that any horse can do? He tries to do it; he says he'll bring me down and humble me, and he puts me to just the hardest, meanest and dir- tiest work, on purpose.

ELIZA:

Oh, George! George! you frighten me. Why, I never heard you talk so. I'm afraid you'll do something dreadful. I don't wonder at your feelings at all; but oh! do be careful — for my sake, for Harry's.

GEORGE:

I have been careful, and I have been patient, but it's growing worse and worse — flesh and blood can't bear it any longer. Every chance he can get to insult and torment me he takes. He says that though I don't say anything, he sees that I've got the devil in me, and he means to bring it out; and one of these days it will come out, in a way that he won't like, or I'm mistaken.

ELIZA:

Well, I always thought that I must obey my master and mistress, or I couldn't be a Christian.

GEORGE:

There is some sense in it in your case. They have brought you up like a child — fed you, clothed you and taught you, so that you have a good education — that is some reason why they should claim you. But I have been kicked and cuffed and sworn at, and what do I owe? I've paid for all my keeping a hundred times over. I won't bear it! — no, I won't! Master will find out that I'm one whipping won't tame. My day will come yet, if he don't look out!

ELIZA:

What are you going to do? Oh! George, don't do anything wicked; if you only trust in heaven and try to do right, it will deliver you.

GEORGE:

Eliza, my heart's full of bitterness. I can't trust in heaven. Why does it let things be so?

ELIZA:

Oh, George! we must all have faith. Mistress says that when all things go wrong to us, we must believe that heaven is doing the very best.

GEORGE:

That's easy for people to say who are sitting on their sofas and riding in their carriages; but let them be where I am — I guess it would come some harder. I wish I could be good; but my heart burns and can't be reconcil- ed. You couldn't, in my place, you can't now, if I tell you all I've got to say; you don't know the whole yet.

ELIZA:

What do you mean?

GEORGE:

Well, lately my master has been saying that he was a fool to let me marry off the place — that he hates Mr. Shelby and all his tribe — and he says he won't let me come here any more, and that I shall take a wife and settle down on his place.

ELIZA:

But you were married to me by the minister, as much as if you had been a white man.

GEORGE:

Don't you know I can't hold you for my wife if he chooses to part us? That is why I wish I'd never seen you — it would have been better for us both — it would have been better for our poor child if he had never been born.

ELIZA:

Oh! but my master is so kind.

GEORGE:

Yes, but who knows? — he may die, and then Harry may be sold to nobody knows who. What pleasure is it that he is handsome and smart and bright? I tell you, Eliza, that a sword will pierce through your soul for every good and pleasant thing your child is or has. It will make him worth too much for you to keep.

ELIZA:

Heaven forbid!

GEORGE:

So, Eliza, my girl, bear up now, and good by, for I'm going.

ELIZA:

Going, George! Going where?

GEORGE:

To Canada; and when I'm there I'll buy you — that's all the hope that's left us. You have a kind master, that won't refuse to sell you. I'll buy you and the boy — heaven helping me, I will!

ELIZA:

Oh, dreadful! If you should be taken?

GEORGE:

I won't be taken, Eliza — I'll die first! I'll be free, or I'll die.

ELIZA:

You will not kill yourself?

GEORGE:

No need of that; they will kill me, fast enough. I will never go down the river alive.

ELIZA:

Oh, George! for my sake, do be careful. Don't lay hands on yourself, or anybody else. You are tempted too much, but don't. Go, if youmust, but go carefully, prudently, and pray heaven to help you!

GEORGE:

Well, then Eliza, hear my plan. I'm going home quite resigned, you understand, as if all was over. I've got some preparations made, and there are those that will help me; and in the course of a few days I shall be among the missing. Well, now, good by.

ELIZA:

A moment — our boy.

GEORGE:

[(Choked with emotion. )]

True, I had forgotten him; one last look, and then farewell!

ELIZA:

And heaven grant it be not forever!

[(Exeunt. )]

## SCENE II

[A dining room. Table and chairs. Dessert, wine, etc., on table. Shelby and Haleydiscovered at table. ]

SHELBY:

That is the way I should arrange the matter.

HALEY:

I can't make trade that way — I positively can't, Mr. Shelby. [(Drinks. )]

SHELBY:

Why, the fact is, Haley, Tom is an uncommon fellow! He is certainly worth that sum anywhere — steady, honest, capable, manages my wholefarm like a clock!

HALEY:

You mean honest, as niggers go. [(Fills glass. )]

SHELBY:

No; I mean, really, Tom is a good, steady, sensible, pious fellow. He got religion at a camp-meeting, four years ago, and I believe he really did get it. I've trusted him since then, with everything I have — money, house, horses, and let him come and go round the country, and I always found him trueand square in everything.

HALEY:

Some folks don't believe there is pious niggers, Shelby, but I do. Ihad a fellow, now, in this yer last lot I took to Orleans — 'twas as good as ameetin' now, really, to hear that critter pray; and he was quite gentle and quietlike. He fetched me a good sum, too, for I bought him cheap of a man that was'bliged to sell out, so I realized six hundred on him. Yes, I consider religion avaleyable thing in a nigger, when it's the genuine article and no mistake.

SHELBY:

Well, Tom's got the real article, if ever a fellow had. Why last fallI let him go to Cincinnati alone, to do business for me and bring home five hun-dred dollars. "Tom, " says I to him, "I trust you, because I think you are a Chris-tian — I know you wouldn't cheat. " Tom comes back sure enough, I knew hewould. Some low fellows, they say, said to him — "Tom, why don't you maketracks for Canada? "

"Ah, master trusted me, and I couldn't, " was his answer. They told me all about it. I am sorry to part with Tom, I must say. You ought tolet him cover the whole balance of the debt and you would, Haley, if you hadany conscience.

HALEY:

Well, I've got just as much conscience as any man in business can affordto keep, just a little, you know, to swear by, as twere; and then I'm ready to doanything in reason to 'blige friends, but this yer, you see, is a leetle too hard on afellow — a leetle too hard! [(Fills glass again. )]

SHELBY:

Well, then, Haley, how will you trade?

HALEY:

Well, haven't you a boy or a girl that you could throw in withTom?

SHELBY:

Hum! none that I could well spare; to tell the truth, it's only hardnecessity makes me willing to sell at all. I don't like parting with any of myhands, that's a fact. [(Harry runs in. )]Hulloa! Jim Crow! [(Throws a bunch ofraisins towards him. )]Pick that up now! [(Harry does so. )]

HALEY:

Bravo, little 'un! [(Throws an orange, which Harry catches. He sings anddances around the stage. )]Hurrah! Bravo! What a young 'un! That chap's a case, I'll promise. Tell you what, Shelby, fling in that chap, and I'll settle thebusiness. Come, now, if that ain't doing the thing up about the rightest! [(Eliza enters. Starts on beholding Haley, and gazes fearfully at Harry, who runsand clings to her dress, showing the orange, etc. )]

SHELBY:

Well, Eliza?

ELIZA:

I was looking for Harry, please, sir.

SHELBY:

Well, take him away, then. [(Eliza grasps the child eagerly in her arms, and casting another glance of apprehen-sion at Haley, exits hastily. )]

HALEY:

By Jupiter! there's an article, now. You might make your fortune onthat ar gal in Orleans any day. I've seen over a thousand in my day, paid downfor gals not a bit handsomer.

SHELBY:

I don't want to make my fortune on her. Another glass of wine. [(Fills the glasses. )]

HALEY:

[(Drinks and smacks his lips. )]Capital wine — first chop. Come, how willyou trade about the gal? What shall I say for her? What'll you take?

SHELBY:

Mr. Haley, she is not to be sold. My wife wouldn't part with herfor her weight in gold.

HALEY:

Ay, ay! women always say such things, 'cause they hain't no sort ofcalculation. Just show 'em how many watches, feathers and trinkets one'sweight in gold would buy, and that alters the case, I reckon.

SHELBY:

I tell you, Haley, this must not be spoken of — I say no, and Imean no.

HALEY:

Well, you'll let me have the boy tho'; you must own that I havecome down pretty handsomely for him.

SHELBY:

What on earth can you want with the child?

HALEY:

Why, I've got a friend that's going into this yer branch of thebusiness — wants to buy up handsome boys to raise for the market. Well, whatdo you say?

SHELBY:

I'll think the matter over and talk with my wife.

HALEY:

Oh, certainly, by all means; but I'm in a devil of a hurry and shallwant to know as soon as possible, what I may depend on. [(Rises and puts on his overcoat, which hangs on a chair. Takes hat and whip. )]

SHELBY:

Well, call up this evening, between six and seven, and you shallhave my answer.

*Uncle Tom's Cabin*

**HALEY:**

All right. Take care of yourself, old boy! [(Exit. )]

**SHELBY:**

If anybody had ever told me that I should sell Tom to those rascal-ly traders, I should never have believed it. Now it must come for aught I see, and Eliza's child too. So much for being in debt, heigho! The fellow sees his ad-vantage and means to push it. [(Exit. )]

### SCENE III

[Snowy landscape. Uncle Tom's Cabin. Snow on roof. Practicable door and win- dow. Dark stage. Music. Enter Eliza hastily, with Harry in her arms. ]

**ELIZA:**

My poor boy! they have sold you, but your mother will save you yet! [(Goes to Cabin and taps on window. Aunt Chloe appears at window with a large white night-cap on. )]

**CHLOE:**

Good Lord! what's that? My sakes alive if it ain't Lizy! Get on your clothes, old man, quick! I'm gwine to open the door. [(The door opens and Chloe enters followed by Uncle Tom in his shirt sleeves holding a tallow candle. )]

**TOM:**

[(Holding the light towards Eliza. )] Lord bless you! I'm skeered to look at ye, Lizy! Are ye tuck sick, or what's come over ye?

**ELIZA:**

I'm running away, Uncle Tom and Aunt Chloe, carrying off my child! Master sold him!

11

TOM & CHLOE:

Sold him!

ELIZA:

Yes, sold him! I crept into the closet by mistress' door tonight and heard master tell mistress that he had sold my Harry and you, Uncle Tom, both, to a trader, and that the man was to take possession tomorrow.

CHLOE:

The good lord have pity on us! Oh! it don't seem as if it was true. What has he done that master should sell him?

ELIZA:

He hasn't done anything — it isn't for that. Master don't want to sell, and mistress — she's always good. I heard her plead and beg for us, but he told her 'twas no use — that he was in this man's debt, and he had got the power over him, and that if he did not pay him off clear, it would end in his having to sell the place and all the people and move off.

CHLOE:

Well, old man, why don't you run away, too? Will you wait to be toted down the river, where they kill niggers with hard work and starving? I'd a heap rather die than go there, any day! There's time for ye, be off with Lizy — you've got a pass to come and go any time. Come, bustle up, and I'll get your things together.

TOM:

No, no — I ain't going. Let Eliza go — it's her right. I wouldn't be the one to say no — 'tain't in natur' for her to stay; but you heard what she said? If I must be sold, or all the people on the place, and everything go to rack, why, let me be sold. I s'pose I can bar it as well as any one. Mas'r always found me on the spot — he always will. I never have broken trust, nor used my pass no ways con- trary to my word, and I never will. It's better for me to go alone, than to break up the place and sell all. Mas'r ain't to blame, and he'll take care of you and the poor little 'uns! [(Overcome. )]

CHLOE:

Now, old man, what is you gwine to cry for? Does you want to break this old woman's heart? [(Crying. )]

ELIZA:

I saw my husband only this afternoon, and I little knew then what was to come. He told me he was going to run away. Do try, if you can, to get word to him. Tell him how I went and why I went, and tell him I'm going to try and find Canada. You must give my love to him, and tell him if I never see him again on earth, I trust we shall meet in heaven!

TOM:

Dat is right, Lizy, trust in the Lord — he is our best friend — our only comforter.

ELIZA:

You won't go with me, Uncle Tom?

TOM:

No; time was when I would, but the Lord's given me a work among these yer poor souls, and I'll stay with 'em and bear my cross with 'em till the end. It's different with you — it's more'n you could stand, and you'd better go if you can.

ELIZA:

Uncle Tom, I'll try it!

TOM:

Amen! The lord help ye! [(Exit Eliza and Harry. )]

CHLOE:

What is you gwine to do, old man! What's to become of you?

TOM:

[(Solemnly. )] Him that saved Daniel in the den of lions — that saved the children in the fiery furnace — Him that walked on the sea and bade the winds be still — He's alive yet! and I've faith to believe he can deliver me.

CHLOE:

You is right, old man.

TOM:

The Lord is good unto all that trust him, Chloe. [(Exeunt into cabin.)]

SCENE IV

[Room in Tavern by the river side. A large window in flat, through which the river is seen, filled wth floating ice. Moon light. Table and chairs brought on. Enter Phineas. ]

PHINEAS:

Chaw me up into tobaccy ends! how in the name of all that's onpossible am I to get across that yer pesky river? It's a reg'lar blockade of ice! I promised Ruth to meet her to-night, and she'll be into my har if I don't come. [(Goes to window. )] Thar's a conglomerated prospect for a loveyer! What in creation's to be done? That thar river looks like a permiscuous ice-cream shop come to an awful state of friz. If I war on the adjacent bank, I wouldn't care a teetotal atom. Rile up, you old varmit, and shake the ice off your back! [Enter: (Enter Eliza and Harry. )]

ELIZA:

Courage, my boy — we have reached the river. Let it but roll between us and our pursuers, and we are safe! [(Goes to window. )] Gracious powers! the river is choked with cakes of ice!

PHINEAS:

Holloa, gal! — what's the matter? You look kind of streaked.

ELIZA:

Is there any ferry or boat that takes people over now?

PHINEAS:

Well, I guess not; the boats have stopped running.

ELIZA:

[(In dismay. )] Stopped running?

PHINEAS:

Maybe you're wanting to get over — anybody sick? Ye seem mighty anxious.

ELIZA:

I — I — I've got a child that's very dangerous. I never heard of it till last night, and I've walked quite a distance to-day, in hopes to get to the ferry.

PHINEAS:

Well, now, that's onlucky; I'm re'lly consarned for ye. Thar's a man, a piece down here, that's going over with some truck this evening, if he duss to; he'll be in here to supper to-night, so you'd better set down and wait. That's a smart little chap. Say, young'un, have a chaw tobaccy? [(Takes out a large plug and a bowie-knife. )]

ELIZA:

No, no! not any for him.

PHINEAS:

Oh! he don't use it, eh? Hain't come to it yet? Well, I have. [(Cuts off a large piece, and returns the plug and knife to pocket. )] What's the matter with the young 'un? He looks kind of white in the gills!

ELIZA:

Poor fellow! he is not used to walking, and I've hurried him on so.

PHINEAS:

Tuckered, eh? Well, there's a little room there, with a fire in it. Take the baby in there, make yourself comfortable till that thar ferryman shows his countenance — I'll stand the damage.

ELIZA:

How shall I thank you for such kindness to a stranger?

PHINEAS:

Well, if you don't know how, why, don't try; that's the teetotal. Come, vamose! [(Exit, Eliza and Harry. )] Chaw me into sassage meat, if that ain't a perpendicular fine gal! she's a reg'lar A No. 1 sort of female! How'n thunder am I to get across this refrigerated stream of water? I can't wait for that ferryman. [(Enter Marks. )] Halloa! what sort of a critter's this? [(Advances. )] Say, stranger, will you have something to drink?

MARKS:

You are excessively kind: I don't care if I do.

PHINEAS:

Ah! he's a human. Holloa, thar! bring us a jug of whisky instantaneously, or expect to be teetotally chawed up! Squat yourself, stranger, and go in for enjoyment. [(They sit at table. )] Who are you, and what's your name?

MARKS:

I am a lawyer, and my name is Marks.

PHINEAS:

A land shark, eh? Well, I dont' think no worse on you for that. The law is a kind of necessary evil; and it breeds lawyers just as an old stump does fungus. Ah! here's the whisky. [(Enter Waiter, with jug and tumblers. Places them on table. )] Here, you — take that shin-plaster. [(Gives bill. )] I don't want any change — thar's a gal stopping in that room — the balance will pay for her — d'ye hear? — vamose! [(Exit Waiter. Fills glass. )] Take hold, neighbor Marks — don't shirk the critter. Here's hoping your path of true love may never have an ice- choked river to cross! [(They drink. )]

MARKS:

Want to cross the river, eh?

PHINEAS:

Well, I do, stranger. Fact is, I'm in love with the teetotalist pretty girl, over on the Ohio side, that ever wore a Quaker bonnet. Take another swig, neighbor. [(Fills glasses, and they drink. )]

MARKS:

A Quaker, eh?

PHINEAS:

Yes — kind of strange, ain't it? The way of it was this: — I used to own a grist of niggers — had 'em to work on my plantation, just below here. Well, stranger, do you know I fell in with that gal — of course I was considerably smashed — knocked into a pretty conglomerated heap — and I told her so. She said she wouldn't hear a word from me so long as I owned a nigger!

MARKS:

You sold them, I suppose?

PHINEAS:

You're teetotally wrong, neighbor. I gave them all their freedom, and told 'em to vamose!

MARKS:

Ah! yes — very noble, I dare say, but rather expensive. This act won you your lady-love, eh?

PHINEAS:

You're off the track again, neighbor. She felt kind of pleased about it, and smiled, and all that; but she said she could never be mine unless I turned Quaker! Thunder and earth! what do you think of that? You're a lawyer — come, now, what's your opinion? Don't you call it a knotty point?

MARKS:

Most decidedly. Of course you refused.

PHINEAS:

Teetotally; but she told me to think better of it, and come to-night and give her my final conclusion. Chaw me into mince meat, if I haven't made up my mind to do it!

MARKS:

You astonish me!

PHINEAS:

Well, you see, I can't get along without that gal; — she's sort of fixed my flint, and I'm sure to hang fire without her. I know I shall make a queer sort of Quaker, because you see, neighbor, I ain't precisely the kind of material to make a Quaker out of.

MARKS:

No, not exactly.

PHINEAS:

Well, I can't stop no longer. I must try to get across that candaverous river some way. It's getting late — take care of yourself, neighbor lawyer. I'm a teetotal victim to a pair of black eyes. Chaw me up to feed hogs, if I'm not in a ruinatious state! [(Exit. )]

MARKS:

Queer genius, that, very! [(Enter Tom Loker. )] So you've come at last.

LOKER:

Yes. [(Looks into jug. )] Empty! Waiter! more whisky! [(Waiter enters, with jug, and removes the empty one. Enter Haley. )]

HALEY:

By the land! if this yer ain't the nearest, now, to what I've heard people call Providence! Why, Loker, how are ye?

LOKER:

The devil! What brought you here, Haley?

HALEY:

[(Sitting at table. )] I say, Tom, this yer's the luckiest thing in the world. I'm in a devil of a hobble, and you must help me out!

LOKER:

Ugh! aw! like enough. A body may be pretty sure of that when you're glad to see 'em, or can make something off of 'em. What's the blow now?

HALEY:

You've got a friend here — partner, perhaps?

LOKER:

Yes, I have. Here, Marks — here's that ar fellow that I was with in Natchez.

MARKS:

[(Grasping Haley's hand. )] Shall be pleased with his acquaintance. Mr. Haley, I believe?

HALEY:

The same, sir. The fact is, gentlemen, this morning I bought a young 'un of Shelby up above here. His mother got wind of it, and what does she do but cut her lucky with him; and I'm afraid by this time that she has crossed the river, for I tracked her to this very place.

MARKS:

So, then, ye're fairly sewed up, ain't ye? He! he! he! it's neatly done, too.

HALEY:

This young 'un business makes lots of trouble in the trade.

MARKS:

Now, Mr. Haley, what is it? Do you want us to undertake to catch this gal?

HALEY:

The gal's no matter of mine — she's Shelby's — it's only the boy. I was a fool for buying the monkey.

LOKER:

You're generally a fool!

MARKS:

Come now, Loker, none of your huffs; you see, Mr. Haley's a-puttin' us in a way of a good job. I reckon: just hold still — these yer arrangements are my forte. This yer gal, Mr. Haley — how is she? what is she? [(Eliza appears, with Harry, listening. )]

HALEY:

Well, white and handsome — well brought up. I'd have given Shelby eight hundred or a thousand, and then made well on her.

MARKS:

White and handsome — well brought up! Look here now, Loker, a beautiful opening. We'll do a business here on our own account. We does the catchin'; the boy, of course, goes to Mr. Haley — we takes the gal to Orleans to speculate on. Ain't it beautiful? [(They confer together. )]

ELIZA:

Powers of mercy, protect me! How shall I escape these human blood-hounds? Ah! the window — the river of ice! That dark stream lies between me and liberty! Surely the ice will bear my trifling weight. It is my only chance of escape — better sink beneath the cold waters, with my child locked in my arms, than have him torn from me and sold into bondage. He sleeps upon my breast — Heaven, I put my trust in thee! [(Gets out of window. )]

MARKS:

Well, Tom Loker, what do you say?

LOKER:

It'll do! [(Strikes his hand violently on the table. Eliza screams. They all start to their feet. Eliza disappears. Music, chord. )]

HALEY:

By the land, there she is now! [(They all rush to the window. )]

MARKS:

She's making for the river!

LOKER:

Let's after her! [(Music. They all leap through the window. Change.)]

SCENE V

[Snow. Landscape. Music. Enter Eliza, with Harry, hurriedly. ]

ELIZA:

They press upon my footsteps — the river is my only hope. Heaven grant me strength to reach it, ere they overtake me! Courage, my child! — we will be free — or perish! [(Rushes off. Music continued. )] [Enter: (Enter Loker, Haley and Marks. )]

HALEY:

We'll catch her yet; the river will stop her!

MARKS:

No, it won't, for look! she has jumped upon the ice! She's brave gal, anyhow!

LOKER:

She'll be drowned!

HALEY:

Curse that young 'un! I shall lose him, after all.

LOKER:

Come on, Marks, to the ferry!

HALEY:

Aye, to the ferry! — a hundred dollars for a boat! [(Music. They rush off. )]

SCENE VI

[The entire depth of stage, representing the Ohio River filled with Floating Ice. Set bank on right and in front. Eliza appears, with Harry, on a cake of ice, and floats slowly across to left. Haley, Loker, and Marks, on bank right, observing. Phineas on opposite shore. ]

END OF ACT I

ACT II

SCENE I

[A Handsome Parlor. Marie discovered reclining on a sofa. ]

MARIE:

[(Looking at a note. )] What can possibly detain St. Clare? According to this note he should have been here a fortnight ago. [(Noise of carriage without. )] I do believe he has come at last. [Enter: (Eva runs in. )]

EVA:

Mamma! [(Throws her arms around Marie's neck, and kisses her. )]

MARIE:

That will do — take care, child — don't you make my head ache! [(Kisses her languidly. )] [Enter: (Enter St. Clare, Ophelia, and Tom, nicely dressed. )]

ST. CLARE:

Well, my dear Marie, here we are at last. The wanderers have arrived, you see. Allow me to present my cousin, Miss Ophelia, who is about to undertake the office of our housekeeper.

MARIE:

[(Rising to a sitting posture. )] I am delighted to see you. How do you like the appearance of our city?

EVA:

[(Running to Ophelia. )] Oh! is it not beautiful? My own darling home! — is it not beautiful?

OPHELIA:

Yes, it is a pretty place, though it looks rather old and heathenish to me.

ST. CLARE:

Tom, my boy, this seems to suit you?

TOM:

Yes, mas'r, it looks about the right thing.

ST. CLARE:

See here, Marie, I've brought you a coachman, at last, to order. I tell you, he is a regular hearse for blackness and sobriety, and will drive you like a funeral, if you wish. Open your eyes, now, and look at him. Now, don't say I never think about you when I'm gone.

MARIE:

I know he'll get drunk.

ST. CLARE:

Oh! no he won't. He's warranted a pious and sober article.

MARIE:

Well, I hope he may turn out well; it's more than I expect, though.

ST. CLARE:

Have you no curiosity to learn how and where I picked up Tom?

EVA:

Uncle Tom papa; that's his name.

ST CLARE:

Right, my little sunbeam!

TOM:

Please, mas'r, that ain't no 'casion to say nothing bout me.

ST. CLARE:

You are too modest, my modern Hannibal. Do you know, Marie, that our little Eva took a fancy to Uncle Tom — whom we met on board the steamboat — and persuaded me to buy him.

MARIE:

Ah! she is so odd.

ST. CLARE:

As we approached the landing, a sudden rush of the passengers precipitated Eva into the water —

MARIE:

Gracious heavens!

ST. CLARE:

A man leaped into the river, and, as she rose to the surface of the water, grasped her in his arms, and held her up until she could be drawn on the boat again. Who was that man, Eva?

EVA:

Uncle, Tom! [(Runs to him. He lifts her in his arms. She kisses him.)]

TOM:

The dear soul!

OPHELIA:

[(Astonished. )] How shiftless!

ST CLARE:

[(Overhearing her. )] What's the matter now, pray?

OPHELIA:

Well, I want to be kind to everybody, and I wouldn't have anything hurt, but as to kissing —

ST. CLARE:

Niggers! that you're not up to, hey?

OPHELIA:

Yes, that's it — how can she?

ST. CLARE:

Oh! bless you, it's nothing when you are used to it!

OPHELIA:

I could never be so shiftless!

EVA:

Come with me, Uncle Tom, and I will show you about the house. [(Crosses with Tom. )]

TOM:

Can I go mas'r?

ST. CLARE:

Yes, Tom; she is your little mistress — your only duty will be to attend to her! [(Tom bows and exits. )]

MARIE:

Eva, my dear!

EVA:

Well, mamma?

MARIE:

Do not exert yourself too much!

EVA:

No, mamma! [(Runs out. )]

OPHELIA:

[(Lifting up her hands. )] How shiftless! [(St. Clare sits next to Marie on sofa. Ophelia next to St. Clare. )]

ST. CLARE:

Well, what do you think of Uncle Tom, Marie?

MARIE:

He is a perfect behemoth!

ST. CLARE:

Come, now, Marie, be gracious, and say something pretty to a fellow!

MARIE:

You've been gone a fortnight beyond the time!

ST. CLARE:

Well, you know I wrote you the reason.

MARIE:

Such a short, cold letter!

ST. CLARE:

Dear me! the mail was just going, and it had to be that or nothing.

MARIE:

That's just the way; always something to make your journeys long and letters short!

ST. CLARE:

Look at this. [(Takes an elegant velvet case from his pocket. )] Here's a present I got for you in New York — a Daguerreotype of Eva and myself.

MARIE:

[(Looks at it with a dissatisfied air. )] What made you sit in such an awk- ward position?

ST. CLARE:

Well, the position may be a matter of opinion, but what do you think of the likeness?

MARIE:

[(Closing the case snappishly. )] If you don't think anything of my opi- nion in one case, I suppose you wouldn't in another.

OPHELIA:

[(Senteniously, aside. )] How shiftless!

ST. CLARE:

Hang the woman! Come, Marie, what do you think of the likeness? Don't be nonsensical now.

MARIE:

It's very inconsiderate of you, St. Calre, to insist on my talking and looking at things. You know I've been lying all day with the sick headache, and there's been such a tumult made ever since you came. I'm half dead!

OPHELIA:

You're subject to the sick headache, ma'am?

MARIE:

Yes, I'm a perfect martyr to it!

OPHELIA:

Juniper-berry tea is good for sick head-ache; at least, Molly, Deacon Abraham Perry's wife, used to say so; and she was a great nurse.

ST. CLARE:

I'll have the first juniper-berries that get ripe in our garden by the lake brought in for that especial purpose. Come, cousin, let us take a stroll in the garden. Will you join us, Marie?

MARIE:

I wonder how you can ask such a question, when you know how fragile I am. I shall retire to my chamber, and repose till dinner time. [(Exit. )]

OPHELIA:

[(Looking after her. )] How shiftless!

ST. CLARE:

Come, cousin! [(As he goes out. )] Look out for the babies! If I step upon anybody, let them mention it.

OPHELIA:

Babies under foot! How shiftless! [(Exeunt. )]

SCENE II

[A Garden. Tom discovered, seated on a bank, with Eva on his knee — his button holes are filled with flowers, and Eva is hanging a wreath around his neck. Music at opening of scene. Enter St. Clare and Ophelia, observing. ]

EVA:

Oh, Tom! you look so funny.

TOM:

[(Sees St. Clare and puts Eva down. )] I begs pardon, mas'r, but the young missis would do it. Look yer, I'm like the ox, mentioned in the good book, dress- ed for the sacrifice.

ST. CLARE:

I say, what do you think, Pussy? Which do you like the best — to live as they do at your uncle's, up in Vermont, or to have a house-full of ser- vants, as we do?

EVA:

Oh! of course our way is the pleasantest.

ST. CLARE:

[(Patting her head. )] Why so?

EVA:

Because it makes so many more round you to love, you know.

OPHELIA:

Now, that's just like Eva — just one of her odd speeches.

EVA:

Is it an odd speech, papa?

ST. CLARE:

Rather, as this world goes, Pussy. But where has my little Eva been?

EVA:

Oh! I've been up in Tom's room, hearing him sing.

ST. CLARE:

Hearing Tom sing, hey?

EVA:

Oh, yes! he sings such beautiful things, about the new Jerusalem, and bright angels, and the land of Canaan.

ST. CLARE:

I dare say; it's better than the opera, isn't it?

EVA:

Yes; and he's going to teach them to me.

ST. CLARE:

Singing lessons, hey? You are coming on.

EVA:

Yes, he sings for me, and I read to him in my Bible, and he explains what it means. Come, Tom. [(She takes his hand and they exit. )]

ST. CLARE:

[(Aside. )] Oh, Evangeline! Rightly named; hath not heaven made thee an evangel to me?

OPHELIA:

How shiftless! How can you let her?

ST. CLARE:

Why not?

OPHELIA:

Why, I don't know; it seems so dreadful.

ST. CLARE:

You would think no harm in a child's caressing a large dog even if he was black; but a creature that can think, reason and feel, and is immortal, you shudder at. Confess it, cousin. I know the feeling among some of you Nor- therners well enough. Not that there is a particle of virtue in our not having it, but custom with us does what Christianity ought to do: obliterates the feelings of personal prejudice. You loathe them as you would a snake or a toad, yet you are indignant at their wrongs. You would not have them abused but you don't want to have anything to do with them yourselves. Isn't that it?

OPHELIA:

Well, cousin, there may be some truth in this.

ST. CLARE:

What would the poor and lowly do without children? Your little child is your only true democrat. Tom, now, is a hero to Eva; his stories are wonders in her eyes; his songs and Methodist hymns are better than an opera, and the traps and little bits of trash in his pockets a mine of jewels, and he the most wonderful Tom that ever wore a black skin. This is one of the roses of Eden that the Lord has dropped down expressly for the poor and lowly, who get few enough of any other kind.

OPHELIA:

It's strange, cousin; one might almost think you was a professor, to hear you talk.

ST. CLARE:

A professor?

OPHELIA:

Yes, a professor of religion.

ST. CLARE:

Not at all; not a professor as you town folks have it, and, what is worse, I'm afraid, not a practicer, either.

OPHELIA:

What makes you talk so, then?

ST. CLARE:

Nothing is easier than talking. My forte lies in talking, and yours, cousin, lies in doing. And speaking of that puts me in mind that I have made a purchase for your department. There's the article now. Here, Topsy! [(Whistles. )] [(Topsy runs on. )]

OPHELIA:

Good gracious! what a heathenish, shiftless looking object! St. Clare, what in the world have you brought that thing here for?

ST. CLARE:

For you to educate, to be sure, and train in the way she should go. I thought she was rather a funny specimen in the Jim Crow line. Here, Top- sy, give us a song, and show us some of your dancing. [(Topsy sings a verse and dances a breakdown. )]

OPHELIA:

[(Paralyzed. )] Well, of all things! If I ever saw the like!

ST. CLARE:

[(Smothering a laugh. )] Topsy, this is your new mistress — I'm going to give you up to her. See now that you behave yourself.

TOPSY:

Yes, mas'r.

ST. CLARE:

You're going to be good, Topsy, you understand?

TOPSY:

Oh, yes, mas'r.

OPHELIA:

Now, St. Clare, what upon earth is this for? Your house is so full of these plagues now, that a body can't set down their foot without treading on 'em. I get up in the morning and find one asleep behind the door, and see one black head poking out from under the table — one lying on the door mat, and they are moping and mowing and grinning between all the railings, and tumbl- ing over the kitchen floor! What on earth did you want to bring this one for?

ST. CLARE:

For you to educate — didn't I tell you? You're always preaching about educating, I thought I would make you a present of a fresh caught specimen, and let you try your hand on her and bring her up in the way she should go.

OPHELIA:

I don't want her, I am sure; I have more to do with 'em now than I want to.

ST. CLARE:

That's you Christians, all over. You'll get up a society, and get some poor missionary to spend all his days among just such heathen; but let me see one of you that would take one into your house with you, and take the labor of their conversion upon yourselves.

OPHELIA:

Well, I didn't think of it in that light. It might be a real mis- sionary work. Well, I'll do what I can. [(Advances to Topsy. )] She's dreadful dirty and shiftless! How old are you, Topsy?

TOPSY:

Dunno, missis.

OPHELIA:

How shiftless! Don't know how old you are? Didn't anybody ever tell you? Who was your mother?

TOPSY:

[(Grinning. )] Never had none.

OPHELIA:

Never had any mother? What do you mean? Where was you born?

TOPSY:

Never was born.

OPHELIA:

You musn't answer me in that way. I'm not playing with you. Tell me where you was born, and who your father and mother were?

TOPSY:

Never was born, tell you; never had no father, nor mother, nor nothin'. I war raised by a speculator, with lots of others. Old Aunt Sue used to take car on us.

ST. CLARE:

She speaks the truth, cousin. Speculators buy them up cheap, when they are little, and get them raised for the market.

OPHELIA:

How long have you lived with your master and mistress?

TOPSY:

Dunno, missis.

OPHELIA:

How shiftless! Is it a year, or more, or less?

TOPSY:

Dunno, missis.

ST. CLARE:

She does not know what a year is; she don't even know her own age.

OPHELIA:

Have you ever heard anything about heaven, Topsy? [(Topsy looks bewildered and grins. )] Do you know who made you?

TOPSY:

Nobody, as I knows on, he, he, he! I spect I growed. Don't think nobody never made me.

OPHELIA:

The shiftless heathen! What can you do? What did you do for your master and mistress?

TOPSY:

Fetch water — and wash dishes — and rub knives — and wait on folks — and dance breakdowns.

OPHELIA:

I shall break down, I'm afraid, in trying to make anything of you, you shiftless mortal!

ST. CLARE:

You find virgin soil there, cousin; put in your own ideas — you won't find many to pull up. [(Exit, laughing. )]

OPHELIA:

[(Takes out her handkerchief. A pair of gloves falls. Topsy picks them up slyly and puts them in her sleeve. )] Follow me, you benighted innocent!

TOPSY:

Yes, missis. [(As Ophelia turns her back to her, she seizes the end of the ribbon she wears around her waist, and twitches it off. Ophelia turns and sees her as she is putting it in her other sleeve. Ophelia takes ribbon from her. )]

OPHELIA:

What's this? You naughty, wicked girl, you've been stealing this?

TOPSY:

Laws! why, that ar's missis' ribbon, a'nt it? How could it got caught in my sleeve?

OPHELIA:

Topsy, you naughty girl, don't you tell me a lie — you stole that ribbon!

TOPSY:

Missis, I declare for't, I didn't — never seed it till dis yer blessed minnit.

OPHELIA:

Topsy, don't you know it's wicked to tell lies?

TOPSY:

I never tells no lies, missis; it's just de truth I've been telling now and nothing else.

OPHELIA:

Topsy, I shall have to whip you, if you tell lies so.

TOPSY:

Laws missis, if you's to whip all day, couldn't say no other way. I never seed dat ar — it must a got caught in my sleeve. [(Blubbers. )]

OPHELIA:

[(Seizes her by the shoulders. )] Don't you tell me that again, you barefaced fibber! [(Shakes her. The gloves fall on stage. )] There you, my gloves too — you outrageous young heathen! [(Picks them up. )] Will you tell me, now, you didn't steal the ribbon?

TOPSY:

No, missis; stole de gloves, but didn't steal de ribbon. It was permiskus.

OPHELIA:

Why, you young reprobate!

TOPSY:

Yes — I's knows I's wicked!

OPHELIA:

Then you know you ought to be punished. [(Boxes her ears. )]

What do you think of that?

TOPSY:

He, he, he! De Lord, missus; dat wouldn't kill a 'skeeter. [(Runs off laughing, Ophelia follows indignantly. )]

SCENE III

[The Tavern by the River. Table and chairs. Jug and glasses on table. On flat is a printed placard, headed: "Four Hundred Dollars Reward — Runaway — George Harris! " Phineas is discovered, seated at table. ]

PHINEAS:

So yer I am; and a pretty business I've undertook to do. Find the hus- band of the gal that crossed the river on the ice two or three days ago. Ruth said I must do it, and I'll be teetotally chawed up if I don't do it. I see they've of- fered a reward for him, dead or alive. How in creation am I to find the varmint? He isn't likely to go round looking natural, with a full description of his hide and figure staring him in the face. [(Enter Mr. Wilson. )] I say, stranger, how are ye? [(Rises and comes forward. )]

WILSON:

Well, I reckon.

PHINEAS:

Any news? [(Takes out plug and knife. )]

WILSON:

Not that I know of.

PHINEAS:

[(Cutting a piece of tobacco and offering it. )] Chaw?

WILSON:

No, thank ye — it don't agree with me.

PHINEAS:

Don't, eh? [(Putting it in his own mouth. )] I never felt any the worse for it.

WILSON:

[(Sees placard. )] What's that?

PHINEAS:

Nigger advertised. [(Advances towards it and spits on it. )] There's my mind upon that.

WILSON:

Why, now, stranger, what's that for?

PHINEAS:

I'd do it all the same to the writer of that ar paper, if he was here. Any man that owns a boy like that, and can't find any better way of treating him, than branding him on the hand with the letter H, as that paper states, deserves to lose him. Such papers as this ar' a shame to old Kaintuck! that's my mind right out, if anybody wants to know.

WILSON:

Well, now, that's a fact.

PHINEAS:

I used to have a gang of boys, sir — that was before I fell in love — and I just told em: — "Boys, " says I, "run now! Dig! put! jest when you want to. I never shall come to look after you! " That's the way I kept mine. Let 'em know they are free to run any time, and it jest stops their wanting to. It stands to reason it should. Treat 'em like men, and you'll have men's work.

WILSON:

I think you are altogether right, friend, and this man described here is a fine fellow — no mistake about that. He worked for me some half dozen years in my bagging factory, and he was my best hand, sir. He is an ingenious fellow, too; he invented a machine for the cleaning of hemp — a really valuable affair; it's gone into use in several factories. His master holds the patent of it.

PHINEAS:

I'll warrant ye; holds it, and makes money out of it, and then turns round and brands the boy in his right hand! If I had a fair chance, I'd mark him, I reckon, so that he'd carry it one while! [Enter: (Enter George Harris, disguised. )]

GEORGE:

[(Speaking as he enters. )] Jim, see to the trunks. [(Sees Wilson. )] Ah! Mr. Wilson here?

WILSON:

Bless my soul, can it be?

GEORGE:

[(Advances and grasps his hand. )] Mr. Wilson, I see you remember me Mr. Butler, of Oaklands. Shelby county.

WILSON:

Ye — yes — yes — sir.

PHINEAS:

Holloa! there's a screw loose here somewhere. That old gentlemen seems to be struck into a pretty considerable heap of astonishment.

May I be teetotally chawed up! if I don't believe that's the identical man I'm arter. [(Crosses to George. )] How are ye, George Harris?

GEORGE:

[(Starting back and thrusting his hands into his breast. )] You know me?

PHINEAS:

Ha, ha, ha! I rather conclude I do; but don't get riled, I an't a bloodhound in disguise.

GEORGE:

How did you discover me?

PHINEAS:

By a teetotal smart guess. You're the very man I want to see. Do you know I was sent after you?

GEORGE:

Ah! by my master?

PHINEAS:

No; by your wife.

GEORGE:

My wife! Where is she?

PHINEAS:

She's stopping with a Quaker family over on the Ohio side.

GEORGE:

Then she is safe?

PHINEAS:

Teetotally!

GEORGE:

Conduct me to her.

PHINEAS:

Just wait a brace of shakes and I'll do it. I've got to go and get the boat ready. 'Twon't take me but a minute — make yourself comfortable till I get back. Chaw me up! but this is what I call doing things in short order. [(Exit. )]

WILSON:

George!

GEORGE:

Yes, George!

WILSON:

I couldn't have thought it!

GEORGE:

I am pretty well disguised, I fancy; you see I don't answer to the advertisment at all.

WILSON:

George, this is a dangerous game you are playing; I could not have advised you to it.

GEORGE:

I can do it on my own responsibility.

WILSON:

Well, George, I suppose you're running away — leaving your lawful master, George, [(I don't wonder at it)] at the same time, I'm sorry, George, yes, decidedly. I think I must say that it's my duty to tell you so.

GEORGE:

Why are you sorry, sir?

WILSON:

Why to see you, as it were, setting yourself in opposition to the laws of your country.

GEORGE:

My country! What country have I, but the grave? And I would to heaven that I was laid there!

WILSON:

George, you've got a hard master, in fact he is — well, he conducts himself reprehensibly — I can't pretend to defend him. I'm sorry for you, now; it's a bad case — very bad; but we must all submit to the indications of pro- vidence. George, don't you see?

GEORGE:

I wonder, Mr. Wilson, if the Indians should come and take you a prisoner away from your wife and children, and want to keep you all your life hoeing corn for them, if you'd think it your duty to abide in the condition in which you were called? I rather imagine that you'd think the first stray horse you could find an indication of providence, shouldn't you?

WILSON:

Really, George, putting the case in that somewhat peculiar light — I don't know — under those circumstances — but what I might. But it seems to me you are running an awful risk. You can't hope to carry it out. If you're taken it will be worse with you than ever; they'll only abuse you, and half kill you, and sell you down river.

GEORGE:

Mr. Wilson, I know all this. I do run a risk, but — [(Throws open coat and shows pistols and knife in his belt. )] There! I'm ready for them. Down South I never will go! no, if it comes to that, I can earn myself at least six feet of free soil — the first and last I shall ever own in Kentucky!

WILSON:

Why, George, this state of mind is awful — it's getting really desperate. I'm concerned. Going to break the laws of your country?

GEORGE:

My country again! Sir, I haven't any country any more than I have any father. I don't want anything of your country, except to be left alone — to go peaceably out of it; but if any man tries to stop me, let him take care, for I am desperate. I'll fight for my liberty, to the last breath I breathe!

You say your fathers did it, if it was right for them, it is right for me!

WILSON:

[(Walking up and down and fanning his face with a large yellow silk handkerchief. )] Blast 'em all! Haven't I always said so — the infernal old cusses! Bless me! I hope I an't swearing now! Well, go ahead, George, go ahead. But be careful, my boy; don't shoot anybody, unless — well, you'd better not shoot — at least I wouldn't hit anybody, you know.

GEORGE:

Only in self-defense.

WILSON:

Well, well. [(Fumbling in his pocket. )] I suppose, perhaps, I an't following my judgment — hang it, I won't follow my judgment. So here, George. [(Takes out a pocket-book and offers George a roll of bills. )]

GEORGE:

No, my kind, good sir, you've done a great deal for me, and this might get you into trouble. I have money enough, I hope, to take me as far as I need it.

WILSON:

No but you must, George. Money is a great help everywhere, can't have too much, if you get it honestly. Take it, do take it, now do, my boy!

GEORGE:

[(Taking the money. )] On condition, sir, that I may repay it at some future time, I will.

WILSON:

And now, George, how long are you going to travel in this way? Not long or far I hope? It's well carried on, but too bold.

GEORGE:

Mr. Wilson, it is so bold, and this tavern is so near, that they will never think of it; they will look for me on ahead, and you yourself wouldn't know me.

WILSON:

But the mark on your hand?

GEORGE:

[(Draws off his glove and shows scar. )] That is a parting mark of Mr. Harris' regard. Looks interesting, doesn't it? [(Puts on glove again. )]

WILSON:

I declare, my very blood runs cold when I think of it — your condition and your risks!

GEORGE:

Mine has run cold a good many years; at present, it's about up to the boiling point.

WILSON:

George, something has brought you out wonderfully. You hold up your head, and move and speak like another man.

GEORGE:

[(Proudly. )] Because I'm a freeman! Yes, sir; I've said "master" for the last time to any man. I'm free!

WILSON:

Take care! You are not sure; you may be taken.

GEORGE:

All men are free and equal in the grave, if it comes to that, Mr. Wilson. [Enter: (Enter Phineas. )]

PHINEAS:

Them's my sentiment, to a teetotal atom, and I don't care who knows it! Neighbor, the boat is ready, and the sooner we make tracks the better. I've seen some mysterious strangers lurking about these diggings, so we'd better put.

GEORGE:

Farewell, Mr. Wilson, and heaven reward you for the many kindnesses you have shown the poor fugitive!

WILSON:

[(Grasping his hand. )] Your're a brave fellow, George. I wish in my heart you were safe through, though — that's what I do.

PHINEAS:

And ain't I the man of all creation to put him through, stranger? Chaw me up if I don't take him to his dear little wife, in the smallest possible quantity of time. Come, neighbor, let's vamose.

GEORGE:

Farewell, Mr. Wilson.

WILSON:

My best wishes go with you, George. [(Exit. )]

PHINEAS:

You're a trump, old Slow-and-Easy.

GEORGE:

[(Looking off. )] Look! look!

PHINEAS:

Consarn their picters, here they come! We can't get out of the house without their seeing us. We're teetotally treed!

GEORGE:

Let us fight our way through them!

PHINEAS:

No, that won't do; there are too many of them for a fair fight — we should be chawed up in no time. [(Looks round and sees trap door.)]

Holloa! here's a cellar door. Just you step down here a few minutes, while I parley with them. [(Lifts trap. )]

GEORGE:

I am resolved to perish sooner than surrender! [(Goes down trap. )]

PHINEAS:

That's your sort! [(Closes trap and stands on it. )] Here they are! [Enter: (Enter Haley, Marks, Loker and three Men. )]

HALEY:

Say, stranger, you haven't seen a runaway darkey about these parts, eh?

PHINEAS:

What kind of a darkey?

HALEY:

A mulatto chap, almost as light-complexioned as a white man.

PHINEAS:

Was he a pretty good-looking chap?

HALEY:

Yes.

PHINEAS:

Kind of tall?

HALEY:

Yes.

PHINEAS:

With brown hair?

HALEY:

Yes.

PHINEAS:

And dark eyes?

HALEY:

Yes.

PHINEAS:

Pretty well dressed?

HALEY:

Yes.

PHINEAS:

Scar on his right hand?

HALEY:

Yes, yes.

PHINEAS:

Well, I ain't seen him.

HALEY:

Oh, bother! Come, boys, let's search the house. [(Exeunt. )]

PHINEAS:

[(Raises trap. )] Now, then, neighbor George. [(George enters up trap. )]

Now's the time to cut your lucky.

GEORGE:

Follow me, Phineas. [(Exit. )]

PHINEAS:

In a brace of shakes. [(Is closing trap as Haley, Marks, Loker, etc., re-enter. )]

HALEY:

Ah! he's down in the cellar. Follow me, boys! [(Thrusts Phineas aside, and rushes down trap, followed by the others. Phineas closes trap and stands on it. )]

PHINEAS:

Chaw me up! but I've got 'em all in a trap. [(Knocking below. )] Be quiet, you pesky varmints! [(Knocking. )] They're getting mighty oneasy. [( Knock- ing. )] Will you be quiet, you savagerous critters! [(The trap is forced open. Haley and Marks appear. Phineas seizes a chair and stands over trap — picture. )] Down with you or I'll smash you into apple-fritters! [(Tableau — closed in. )]

SCENE IV

[A Plain chamber. ]

TOPSY:

[(Without. )] You go 'long. No more nigger dan you be! [(Enters, shouts and laughter without — looks off. )] You seem to think yourself white folks. You ain't nerry one — black nor white. I'd like to be one or turrer. Law! you niggers, does you know you's all sinners? Well, you is — everybody is. White folks is sin- ners too — Miss Feely says so — but I 'spects niggers is the biggest ones. But Lor! ye ain't any on ye up to me. I's so awful wicked there can't nobody do nothin' with me. I used to keep old missis a-swarin' at me ha' de time. I 'spects I's de wickedest critter in de world. [(Song and dance introduced. Enter Eva. )]

EVA:

Oh, Topsy! Topsy! you have been very wrong again.

TOPSY:

Well, I 'spects I have.

EVA:

What makes you do so?

TOPSY:

I dunno; I 'spects it's cause I's so wicked.

EVA:

Why did you spoil Jane's earrings?

TOPSY:

'Cause she's so proud. She called me a little black imp, and turned up her pretty nose at me 'cause she is whiter than I am. I was gwine by her room, and I seed her coral earrings lying on de table, so I threw dem on de floor, and put my foot on 'em, and scrunches 'em all to little bits — he! he! he! I's so wicked.

EVA:

Don't you know that was very wrong?

TOPSY:

I don't car'! I despises dem what sets up for fine ladies, when dey ain't nothing but cream-colored niggers! Dere's Miss Rosa — she gives me lots of 'pertinent remarks. T'other night she was gwine to a ball. She put on a beau'ful dress dat missis give her — wid her har curled, all nice and pretty. She hab to go down de back stairs — dem am dark — and I puts a pail of hot water on dem, and she put her foot into it, and den she go tumbling to de bottom of de stairs, and de water go all ober her, and spile her dress, and scald her dreadful bad! He! he! he! I's so wicked!

EVA:

Oh! how could you!

TOPSY:

Don't dey despise me cause I don't know nothing? Don't dey laugh at me 'cause I'm brack, and dey ain't?

EVA:

But you shouldn't mind them.

TOPSY:

Well, I don't mind dem; but when dey are passing under my winder, I trows dirty water on'em, and dat spiles der complexions.

EVA:

What does make you so bad, Topsy? Why won't you try and be good? Don't you love anybody, Topsy?

TOPSY:

Can't recommember.

EVA:

But you love your father and mother?

TOPSY:

Never had none, ye know, I told ye that, Miss Eva.

EVA:

Oh! I know; but hadn't you any brother, or sister, or aunt, or —

TOPSY:

No, none on 'em — never had nothing nor nobody. I's brack — no one loves me!

EVA:

Oh! Topsy, I love you! [(Laying her hand on Topsy's shoulder. )] I love you because you haven't had any father, or mother, or friends. I love you, I want you to be good. I wish you would try to be good for my sake. [(Topsy looks astonished for a moment, and then bursts into tears. )] Only think of it, Top- sy — you can be one of those spirits bright Uncle Tom sings about!

TOPSY:

Oh! dear Miss Eva — dear Miss Eva! I will try — I will try. I never did care nothin' about it before.

EVA:

If you try, you will succeed. Come with me. [(Crosses and takes Topsy's hand. )]

TOPSY:

I will try; but den, I's so wicked! [(Exit Eva followed by Topsy, crying. )]

SCENE V

[Enter: Chamber. Enter George, Eliza and Harry. ]

GEORGE:

At length, Eliza, after many wanderings, we are united.

ELIZA:

Thanks to these generous Quakers, who have so kindly sheltered us.

GEORGE:

Not forgetting our friend Phineas.

ELIZA:

I do indeed owe him much. 'Twas he I met upon the icy river's bank, after that fearful, but successful attempt, when I fled from the slave-trader with my child in my arms.

GEORGE:

It seems almost incredible that you could have crossed the river on the ice.

ELIZA:

Yes, I did. Heaven helping me, I crossed on the ice, for they were behind me — right behind — and there was no other way.

GEORGE:

But the ice was all in broken-up blocks, swinging and heaving up and down in the water.

ELIZA:

I know it was — I know it; I did not think I should get over, but I did not care — I could but die if I did not! I leaped on the ice, but how I got across I don't know; the first I remember, a man was helping me up the bank — that man was Phineas.

GEORGE:

My brave girl! you deserve your freedom — you have richly earned it!

ELIZA:

And when we get to Canada I can help you to work, and between us we can find something to live on.

GEORGE:

Yes, Eliza, so long as we have each other, and our boy. Oh, Eliza, if these people only knew what a blessing it is for a man to feel that his wife and child belong to him! I've often wondered to see men that could call their wives and children their own, fretting and worrying about anything else. Why, I feel rich and strong, though we have nothing but our bare hands. If they will only let me alone now, I will be satisfied — thankful!

ELIZA:

But we are not quite out of danger; we are not yet in Canada.

GEORGE:

True, but it seems as if I smelt the free air, and it makes me strong! [Enter: (Enter Phineas, dressed as a Quaker. )]

PHINEAS:

[(With a snuffle. )] Verily, friends, how is it with thee? — hum!

GEORGE:

Why, Phineas, what means this metamorphosis?

PHINEAS:

I've become a Quaker, that's the meaning on't.

GEORGE:

What — you?

PHINEAS:

Teetotally! I was driven to it by a strong argument, composed of a pair of sparkling eyes, rosy cheeks, and pouting lips. Them lips would per- suade a man to assassinate his grandmother! [(Assumes the Quaker tone again. )]

Verily, George, I have discovered something of importance to the interests of thee and thy party, and it were well for thee to hear it.

GEORGE:

Keep us not in suspense!

PHINEAS:

Well, after I left you on the road, I stopped at a little, lone tavern, just below here. Well, I was tired with hard driving, and after my supper I stret- ched myself down on a pile of bags in the corner, and pulled a buffalo hide over me — and what does I do but get fast asleep.

GEORGE:

With one ear open, Phineas?

PHINEAS:

No, I slept ears and all for an hour or two, for I was pretty well tired; but when I came to myself a little, I found that there were some men in the room, sitting round a table, drinking and talking; and I thought, before I made much muster, I'd just see what they were up to, especially as I heard them say something about the Quakers. Then I listened with both ears and found they were talking about you. So I kept quiet, and heard them lay off all their plans. They've got a right notion of the track we are going to-night, and they'll be down after us, six or eight strong. So, now, what's to be done?

ELIZA:

What shall we do, George?

GEORGE:

I know what I shall do! [(Takes out pistols. )]

PHINEAS:

Ay-ay, thou seest, Eliza, how it will work — pistols — phitz — poppers!

ELIZA:

I see; but I pray it come not to that!

GEORGE:

I don't want to involve any one with or for me. If you will lend me your vehicle, and direct me, I will drive alone to the next stand.

PHINEAS:

Ah! well, friend, but thee'll need a driver for all that. Thee's quite welcome to do all the fighting thee knows; but I know a thing or two about the road that thee doesn't

GEORGE:

But I don't want to involve you.

PHINEAS:

Involve me! Why, chaw me — that is to say — when thee does involve me, please to let me know.

ELIZA:

Phineas is a wise and skillful man. You will do well, George, to abide by his judgment. And, oh! George, be not hasty with these — young blood is hot! [(Laying her hand on pistols. )]

GEORGE:

I will attack no man. All I ask of this country is to be left alone, and I will go out peaceably. But I'll fight to the last breath before they shall take from me my wife and son! Can you blame me?

PHINEAS:

Mortal man cannot blame thee, neighbor George! Flesh and blood could not do otherwise. Woe unto the world because of offenses, but woe unto them through whom the offense cometh! That's gospel, teetotally!

GEORGE:

Would not even you, sir, do the same, in my place?

PHINEAS:

I pray that I be not tried; the flesh is weak — but I think my flesh would be pretty tolerably strong in such a case; I ain't sure, friend George, that I shouldn't hold a fellow for thee, if thee had any accounts to settle with him.

ELIZA:

Heaven grant we be not tempted.

PHINEAS:

But if we are tempted too much, why, consarn 'em! let them look out, that's all.

GEORGE:

It's quite plain you was not born for a Quaker. The old nature has its way in you pretty strong yet.

PHINEAS:

Well, I reckon you are pretty teetotally right.

GEORGE:

Had we not better hasten our flight?

PHINEAS:

Well, I rather conclude we had; we're full two hours ahead of them, if they start at the time they planned; so let's vamose. [(Exeunt. )]

## SCENE VI

[A Rocky Pass in the Hills. Large set rock and platform. ]

PHINEAS:

[(Without. )] Out with you in a twinkling, every one, and up into these rocks with me! run now, if you ever did run! [(Music. Phineas enters, with Harry in his arms. George supporting Eliza. )] Come up here; this is one of our old hunting dens. Come up. [(They ascend the rock. )] Well, here we are. Let 'em get us if they can. Whoever comes here has to walk single file between those two rocks, in fair range of your pistols — d'ye see?

GEORGE:

I do see. And now, as this affair is mine, let me take all the risk, and do all the fighting.

PHINEAS:

Thee's quite welcome to do the fighting, George; but I may have the fun of looking on, I suppose. But see, these fellows are kind of debating down there, and looking up, like hens when they are going to fly up onto the roost. Hadn't thee better give 'em a word of advice, before they come up, just to tell 'em handsomely they'll be shot if they do. [Enter: (Loker, Marks, and three Men enter. )]

MARKS:

Well, Tom, your coons are fairly treed.

LOKER:

Yes, I see 'em go up right here; and here's a path — I'm for going right up. They can't jump down in a hurry, and it won't take long to ferret 'em out.

MARKS:

But, Tom, they might fire at us from behind the rocks. That would be ugly, you know.

LOKER:

Ugh! always for saving your skin, Marks. No danger, niggers are too plaguy scared!

MARKS:

I don't know why I shouldn't save my skin, it's the best I've got; and niggers do fight like the devil sometimes.

GEORGE:

[(Rising on the rock. )] Gentlemen, who are you down there and what do you want?

LOKER:

We want a party of runaway niggers. One George and Eliza Har- ris, and their son. We've got the officers here, and a warrant to take 'em too. D'ye hear? An't you George Harris, that belonged to Mr. Harris, of Shelby county, Kentucky?

GEORGE:

I am George Harris. A Mr. Harris, of Kentucky, did call me his property. But now I'm a freeman, standing on heaven's free soil! My wife and child I claim as mine. We have arms to defend ourselves and we mean to do it. You can come up if you like, but the first one that comes within range of our bullets is a dead man!

MARKS:

Oh, come — come, young man, this ar no kind of talk at all for you. You see we're officers of justice. We've got the law on our side, and the power and so forth; so you'd better give up peaceably, you see — for you'll certainly have to give up at last.

GEORGE:

I know very well that you've got the law on your side, and the power; but you haven't got us. We are standing here as free as you are, and by the great power that made us, we'll fight for our liberty till we die! [(During this, Marks draws a pistol, and when he concludes fires at him. Eliza screams. )] It's nothing, Eliza; I am unhurt.

PHINEAS:

[(Drawing George down. )] Thee'd better keep out of sight with thy speechifying; they're teetotal mean scamps.

LOKER:

What did you do that for, Marks?

MARKS:

You see, you get jist as much for him dead as alive in Kentucky.

GEORGE:

Now, Phineas, the first man that advances I fire at; you take the second and so on. It won't do to waste two shots on one.

PHINEAS:

But what if you don't hit?

GEORGE:

I'll try my best.

PHINEAS:

Creation! chaw me up if there a'nt stuff in you!

MARKS:

I think I must have hit some on'em. I heard a squeal.

LOKER:

I'm going right up for one. I never was afraid of niggers, and I an't a going to be now. Who goes after me? [(Music. Loker dashes up the rock. George fires. He staggers for a moment, then springs to the top. Phineas seizes him. A struggle. )]

PHINEAS:

Friend, thee is not wanted here! [(Throws Loker over the rock. )]

MARKS:

[(Retreating. )] Lord help us — they're perfect devils! [(Music. Marks and Party run off. George and Eliza kneel in an attitude of thanksgiving, with the Child between them. Phineas stands over them exulting. Tableau. )]

## END OF ACT II

## ACT III

### SCENE I

[Chamber. Enter St. Clare, followed by Tom. ]

ST. CLARE:

[(Giving money and papers to Tom. )] There, Tom, are the bills, and the money to liquidate them.

TOM:

Yes, mas'r.

ST. CLARE:

Well, Tom, what are you waiting for? Isn't all right there?

TOM:

I'm fraid not, mas'r.

ST. CLARE:

Why, Tom, what's the matter? You look as solemn as a judge.

TOM:

I feel very bad, mas'r. I allays have thought that mas'r would be good to everybody.

ST. CLARE:

Well, Tom, haven't I been? Come, now, what do you want? There's something you haven't got, I suppose, and this is the preface.

TOM:

Mas'r allays been good to me. I haven't nothing to complain of on that head; but there is one that mas'r isn't good to.

ST. CLARE:

Why, Tom, what's got into you? Speak out — what do you mean?

TOM:

Last night, between one and two, I thought so. I studied upon the matter then — mas'r isn't good to himself.

ST. CLARE:

Ah! now I understand; you allude to the state in which I came home last night. Well, to tell the truth, I was slightly elevated — a little more champagne on board than I could comfortably carry. That's all, isn't it?

TOM:

[(Deeply affected — clasping his hands and weeping. )] All! Oh! my dear young mas'r, I'm 'fraid it will be loss of all — all, body and soul. The good book says "it biteth like a serpent and stingeth like an adder, " my dear mas'r.

ST. CLARE:

You poor, silly fool! I'm not worth crying over.

TOM:

Oh, mas'r! I implore you to think of it before it gets too late.

ST. CLARE:

Well, I won't go to any more of their cursed nonsense, Tom — on my honor, I won't. I don't know why I haven't stopped long ago;

I've always despised it, and myself for it. So now, Tom, wipe up your eyes and go about your errands.

TOM:

Bless you, mas'r. I feel much better now. You have taken a load from poor Tom's heart. Bless you!

ST. CLARE:

Come, come, no blessings; I'm not so wonderfully good, now.

There, I'll pledge my honor to you, Tom, you don't see me so again. [(Exit Tom. )]

I'll keep my faith with him, too.

OPHELIA:

[(Without. )] Come along, you shiftless mortal!

ST. CLARE:

What new witchcraft has Topsy been brewing? That commo- tion is of her raising, I'll be bound. [(Enter Ophelia, dragging in Topsy. )]

OPHELIA:

Come here now; I will tell your master.

ST. CLARE:

What's the matter now?

OPHELIA:

The matter is that I cannot be plagued with this girl any longer. It's past all bearing; flesh and blood cannot endure it. Here I locked her up and gave her a hymn to study; and what does she do but spy out where I put my key, and has gone to my bureau, and got a bonnet-trimming and cut it all to pieces to make dolls' jackets! I never saw anything like it in my life!

ST. CLARE:

What have you done to her?

OPHELIA:

What have I done? What haven't I done? Your wife says I ought to have her whipped till she couldn't stand.

ST. CLARE:

I don't doubt it. Tell me of the lovely rule of woman. I never saw above a dozen women that wouldn't half kill a horse or servant, either, if they had their own way with them — let alone a man.

OPHELIA:

I am sure, St. Clare, I don't know what to do. I've taught and taught — I've talked till I'm tired; I've whipped her, I've punished her in every way I could think of, and still she's just what she was at first.

ST. CLARE:

Come here, Tops, you monkey! [(Topsy crosses to St. Clare, grinning. )] What makes you behave so?

TOPSY:

'Spects it's my wicked heart — Miss Feely says so.

ST. CLARE:

Don't you see how much Miss Ophelia has done for you? She says she has done everything she can think of.

TOPSY:

Lord, yes, mas'r! old missis used to say so, too. She whipped me a heap harder, and used to pull my ha'r, and knock my head agin the door; but it didn't do me no good. I 'spects if they's to pull every spear of ha'r out o' my head, it wouldn't do no good neither — I's so wicked! Laws! I's nothin' but a nig- ger, no ways! [(Goes up. )]

OPHELIA:

Well, I shall have to give her up; I can't have that trouble any longer.

ST. CLARE:

I'd like to ask you one question.

OPHELIA:

What is it?

ST. CLARE:

Why, if your doctrine is not strong enough to save one heathen child, that you can have at home here, all to yourself, what's the use of sending one or two poor missionaries off with it among thousands of just such? I suppose this girl is a fair sample of what thousands of your heathen are.

OPHELIA:

I'm sure I don't know; I never saw such a girl as this.

ST. CLARE:

What makes you so bad, Tops? Why won't you try and be good? Don't you love any one, Topsy?

TOPSY:

[(Comes down. )] Dunno nothing 'bout love; I loves candy and sich, that's all.

OPHELIA:

But, Topsy, if you'd only try to be good, you might.

TOPSY:

Couldn't never be nothing but a nigger, if I was ever so good. If I could be skinned and come white, I'd try then.

ST. CLARE:

People can love you, if you are black, Topsy. Miss Ophelia would love you, if you were good. [(Topsy laughs. )] Don't you think so?

TOPSY:

No, she can't b'ar me, 'cause I'm a nigger — she'd's soon have a toad touch her. There can't nobody love niggers, and niggers can't do nothin'! I don't car'! [(Whistles. )]

ST. CLARE:

Silence, you incorrigible imp, and begone!

TOPSY:

He! he! he! didn't get much out of dis chile! [(Exit. )]

OPHELIA:

I've always had a prejudice against negroes, and it's a fact — I never could bear to have that child touch me, but I didn't think she knew it.

ST. CLARE:

Trust any child to find that out, there's no keeping it from them. but I believe all the trying in the world to benefit a child, and all the substantial favors you can do them, will never excite one emotion of gratitude, while that feeling of repugnance remains in the heart. It's a queer kind of a fact, but so it is.

OPHELIA:

I don't know how I can help it — they are disagreeable to me, this girl in particular. How can I help feeling so?

ST. CLARE:

Eva does, it seems.

OPHELIA:

Well, she's so loving. I wish I was like her. She might teach me a lesson.

ST. CLARE:

It would not be the first time a little child had been used to instruct an old disciple, if it were so. Come, let us seek Eva, in her favorite bower by the lake.

OPHELIA:

Why, the dew is falling, she mustn't be out there. She is unwell, I know.

ST. CLARE:

Don't be croaking, cousin — I hate it.

OPHELIA:

But she has that cough.

ST. CLARE:

Oh, nonsense, of that cough — it is not anything. She has taken a little cold, perhaps.

OPHELIA:

Well, that was just the way Eliza Jane was taken — and Ellen —

ST. CLARE:

Oh, stop these hobgoblin, nurse legends. You old hands get so wise, that a child cannot cough or sneeze, but you see desperation and ruin at hand. Only take care of the child, keep her from the night air, and don't let her play too hard, and she'll do well enough. [(Exeunt. )]

## SCENE II

[The flat represents the lake. The rays of the setting sun tinge the waters with gold. A large tree. Beneath this a grassy bank, on which Eva and Tom are seated side by side. Eva has a Bible open on her lap. Music. ]

TOM:

Read dat passage again, please, Miss Eva?

EVA:

[(Reading. )] "And I saw a sea of glass, mingled with fire. " [(Stopping sud- denly and pointing to lake. )] Tom, there it is!

TOM:

What, Miss Eva?

EVA:

Don't you see there? There's a "sea of glass mingled with fire. "

TOM:

True enough, Miss Eva. [(Sings. )]

Oh, had I the wings of the morning, I'd fly away to Canaan's shore; Bright angels should convey me home, To the New Jerusalem.

EVA:

Where do you suppose New Jerusalem is, Uncle Tom?

TOM:

Oh, up in the clouds, Miss Eva.

EVA:

Then I think I see it. Look in those clouds, they look like great gates of pearl; and you can see beyond them — far, far off — it's all gold! Tom, sing about 'spirits bright.'

TOM:

[(Sings.)]

I see a band of spirits bright, That taste the glories there; They are all robed in spotless white, And conquering palms they bear.

EVA:

Uncle Tom, I've seen them.

TOM:

To be sure you have; you are one of them yourself. You are the brightest spirit I ever saw.

EVA:

They come to me sometimes in my sleep — those spirits bright —

They are all robed in spotless white, And conquering palms they bear. Uncle Tom, I'm going there.

TOM:

Where, Miss Eva?

EVA:

[(((Pointing to the sky. )] I'm going there, to the spirits bright, Tom; I'm go- ing before long.

TOM:

It's jest no use tryin' to keep Miss Eva here; I've allays said so. She's got the Lord's mark in her forehead. She wasn't never like a child that's to live — there was always something deep in her eyes. [(Rises and comes forward. Eva also comes forward, leaving Bible on bank.)] [Enter: (Enter St. Clare. )]

ST. CLARE:

Ah! my little pussy, you look as blooming as a rose! You are better now-a-days, are you not?

EVA:

Papa, I've had things I wanted to say to you a great while. I want to say them now, before I get weaker.

ST. CLARE:

Nay, this is an idle fear, Eva; you know you grow stronger every day.

EVA:

It's all no use, papa, to keep it to myself any longer. The time is com- ing that I am going to leave you, I am going, and never to come back.

ST. CLARE:

Oh, now, my dear little Eva! you've got nervous and low spirited; you mustn't indulge such gloomy thoughts.

# Uncle Tom's Cabin

EVA:

No, papa, don't deceive yourself, I am not any better; I know it perfectly well, and I am going before long. I am not nervous — I am not low spirited. If it were not for you, papa, and my friends, I should be perfectly hap- py. I want to go — I long to go!

ST. CLARE:

Why, dear child, what has made your poor little heart so sad? You have everything to make you happy that could be given you.

EVA:

I had rather be in heaven! There are a great many things here that makes me sad — that seem dreadful to me; I had rather be there; but I don't want to leave you — it almost breaks my heart!

ST. CLARE:

What makes you sad, and what seems dreadful, Eva?

EVA:

I feel sad for our poor people; they love me dearly, and they are all good and kind to me. I wish, papa, they were all free!

ST. CLARE:

Why, Eva, child, don't you think they are well enough off now?

EVA:

[(Not heeding the question. )] Papa, isn't there a way to have slaves made free? When I am dead, papa, then you will think of me and do it for my sake?

ST. CLARE:

When you are dead, Eva? Oh, child, don't talk to me so. You are all I have on earth!

77

EVA:

Papa, these poor creatures love their children as much as you do me. Tom loves his children. Oh, do something for them!

ST. CLARE:

There, there, darling; only don't distress yourself, and don't talk of dying, and I will do anything you wish.

EVA:

And promise me, dear father, that Tom shall have his freedom as soon as — [(Hesitating. )] — I am gone!

ST. CLARE:

Yes, dear, I will do anything in the world — anything you could ask me to. There, Tom, take her to her chamber, this evening air is too chill for her. [(Music. Kisses her. Tom takes Eva in his arms, and exits. Gazing mournful- ly after Eva. )] Has there ever been a child like Eva? Yes, there has been; but their names are always on grave-stones, and their sweet smiles, their heavenly eyes, their singular words and ways, are among the buried treasures of yearning hearts. It is as if heaven had an especial band of angels, whose office it is to so- journ for a season here, and endear to them the wayward human heart, that they might bear it upward with them in their homeward flight. When you see that deep, spiritual light in the eye when the little soul reveals itself in words sweeter and wiser than the ordinary words of children, hope not to retain that child; for the seal of heaven is on it, and the light of immortality looks out from its eyes! [(Music. Exit. )]

SCENE III

[Enter: A corridor. Proscenium doors on. Music. Enter Tom, he listens at door and then lies down. Enter Ophelia, with candle. ]

OPHELIA:

Uncle Tom, what alive have you taken to sleeping anywhere and everywhere, like a dog, for? I thought you were one of the orderly sort, that lik- ed to lie in bed in a Christian way.

TOM:

[(Rises. Mysteriously. )] I do, Miss Feely, I do, but now —

OPHELIA:

Well, what now?

TOM:

We mustn't speak loud; Mas'r St. Clare won't hear on't; but Miss Feely, you know there must be somebody watchin' for the bridegroom.

OPHELIA:

What do you mean, Tom?

TOM:

You know it says in Scripture, "At midnight there was a great cry made, behold, the bridegroom cometh! " That's what I'm spectin' now, every night, Miss Feely, and I couldn't sleep out of hearing, noways.

OPHELIA:

Why, Uncle Tom, what makes you think so?

TOM:

Miss Eva, she talks to me. The Lord, he sends his messenger in the soul. I must be thar, Miss Feely; for when that ar blessed child goes into the kingdom, they'll open the door so wide, we'll all get a look in at the glory!

OPHELIA:

Uncle Tom, did Miss Eva say she felt more unwell than usual to-night?

TOM:

No; but she told me she was coming nearer — thar's them that tells it to the child, Miss Feely. It's the angels — it's the trumpet sound afore the break o' day!

OPHELIA:

Heaven grant your fears be vain! Come in, Tom [(Exeunt. )]

SCENE IV

[Eva's Chamber. Eva discovered on a couch. A table stands near the couch with a lamp on it. The light shines upon Eva's face, which is very pale. Scene half dark. Uncle Tom is kneeling near the foot of the couch, Ophelia stands at the head, St. Clare at back. Scene opens to plaintive music. After a strain enter Marie, hastily. ]

MARIE:

St. Clare! Cousin! Oh! what is the matter now?

ST. CLARE:

[(Hoarsely. )] Hush! she is dying!

MARIE:

[(Sinking on her knees, beside Tom. )] Dying!

ST. CLARE:

Oh! if she would only wake and speak once more. [(Bending over Eva. )] Eva, darling! [(Eva uncloses her eyes, smiles, raises her head and tries to speak. )] Do you know me, Eva?

EVA:

[(Throwing her arms feebly about his neck. )] Dear papa. [(Her arms drop and she sinks back. )]

ST. CLARE:

Oh heaven! this is dreadful! Oh! Tom, my boy, it is killing me!

TOM:

Look at her, mas'r. [(Points to Eva. )]

ST. CLARE:

[(A pause. )] She does not hear. Oh Eva! tell us what you see. What is it?

EVA:

[(Feebly smiling. )] Oh! love! joy! peace! [(Dies)]

TOM:

Oh! bless the Lord! it's over, dear mas'r, it's over.

ST. CLARE:

[(Sinking on his knees. )] Farewell, beloved child! the bright eternal doors have closed after thee. We shall see thy sweet face no more. Oh! woe for them who watched thy entrance into heaven when they shall wake and find on- ly the cold, gray sky of daily life and thou gone forever. [(Solemn music, slow curtain. )]

### END OF ACT III

## ACT IV

## SCENE I

[A street in New Orleans. Enter Gumption Cute, meeting Marks. ]

CUTE:

How do ye dew?

MARKS:

How are you?

CUTE:

Well, now, squire, it's a fact that I am dead broke and busted up.

MARKS:

You have been speculating, I suppose!

CUTE:

That's just it and nothing shorter.

MARKS:

You have had poor success, you say?

CUTE:

Tarnation bad, now I tell you. You see I came to this part of the country to make my fortune.

MARKS:

And you did not do it?

CUTE:

Scarcely. The first thing I tried my hand at was keeping school. I opened an academy for the instruction of youth in the various branches of or- thography, geography, and other graphies.

MARKS:

Did you succeed in getting any pupils?

CUTE:

Oh, lots on 'em! and a pretty set of dunces they were too. After the first quarter, I called on the repectable parents of the juveniles, and requested them to fork over. To which they politely answered — don't you wish you may get it?

MARKS:

What did you do then?

CUTE:

Well, I kind of pulled up stakes and left those diggins. Well then I went into Spiritual Rappings for a living. That paid pretty well for a short time, till I met with an accident.

MARKS:

An accident?

CUTE:

Yes; a tall Yahoo called on me one day, and wanted me to summon the spirit of his mother — which, of course, I did. He asked me about a dozen questions which I answered to his satisfaction. At last he wanted to know what she died of — I said, Cholera. You never did see a critter so riled as he was. 'Look yere, stranger, ' said he, 'it's my opinion that you're a pesky humbug! for my mother was blown up in a Steamboat! ' with that he left the premises. The next day the people furnished me with a conveyance, and I rode out of town.

MARKS:

Rode out of town?

CUTE:

Yes; on a rail!

MARKS:

I suppose you gave up the spirits, after that?

CUTE:

Well, I reckon I did; it had such an effect on my spirits.

MARKS:

It's a wonder they didn't tar and feather you.

CUTE:

There was some mention made of that, but when they said feathers, I felt as if I had wings and flew away.

MARKS:

You cut and run?

CUTE:

Yes; I didn't like their company and I cut it. Well, after that I let myself out as an overseer on a cotton plantation. I made a pretty good thing of that, though it was dreadful trying to my feelings to flog the darkies; but I got used to it after a while, and then I used to lather 'em like Jehu. Well, the pro- prietor got the fever and ague and shook himself out of town. The place and all the fixings were sold at auction and I found myself adrift once more.

MARKS:

What are you doing at present?

CUTE:

I'm in search of a rich relation of mine.

MARKS:

A rich relation?

CUTE:

Yes, a Miss Ophelia St. Clare. You see, a niece of hers married one of my second cousins — that's how I came to be a relation of hers. She came on here from Vermont to be housekeeper to a cousin of hers, of the same name.

MARKS:

I know him well.

CUTE:

The deuce you do! — well, that's lucky.

MARKS:

Yes, he lives in this city.

CUTE:

Say, you just point out the locality, and I'll give him a call.

MARKS:

Stop a bit. Suppose you shouldn't be able to raise the wind in that quarter, what have you thought of doing?

CUTE:

Well, nothing particular.

MARKS:

How should you like to enter into a nice, profitable business — one that pays well?

CUTE:

That's just about my measure — it would suit me to a hair. What is it?

MARKS:

Nigger catching.

CUTE:

Catching niggers! What on airth do you mean?

MARKS:

Why, when there's a large reward offered for a runaway darkey, we goes after him, catches him, and gets the reward.

CUTE:

Yes, that's all right so far — but s'pose there ain't no reward offered?

MARKS:

Why, then we catches the darkey on our own account, sells him, and pockets the proceeds.

CUTE:

By chowder, that ain't a bad speculation!

MARKS:

What do you say? I want a partner. You see, I lost my partner last year, up in Ohio — he was a powerful fellow.

CUTE:

Lost him! How did you lose him?

MARKS:

Well, you see, Tom and I — his name was Tom Loker — Tom and I were after a mulatto chap, called George Harris, that run away from Kentucky. We traced him though the greater part of Ohio, and came up with him near the Pennsylvania line. He took refuge among some rocks, and showed fight.

CUTE:

Oh! then runaway darkies show fight, do they?

MARKS:

Sometimes. Well, Tom — like a headstrong fool as he was — rushed up the rocks, and a Quaker chap, who was helping this George Harris, threw him over the cliff.

CUTE:

Was he killed?

MARKS:

Well, I didn't stop to find out. Seeing that the darkies were stronger than I thought, I made tracks for a safe place.

CUTE:

And what became of this George Harris?

MARKS:

Oh! he and his wife and child got away safe into Canada. You see, they will get away sometimes though it isn't very often. Now what do you say? You are just the figure for a fighting partner. Is it a bargain?

CUTE:

Well, I rather calculate our teams won't hitch, no how. By chowder, I hain't no idea of setting myself up as a target for darkies to fire at — that's a speculation that don't suit my constitution.

MARKS:

You're afraid, then?

CUTE:

No, I ain't, it's against my principles.

MARKS:

Your principles — how so?

CUTE:

Because my principles are to keep a sharp lookout for No. 1. I shouldn't feel wholesome if a darkie was to throw me over that cliff to look after Tom Loker. [(Extent arm-in-arm. )]

SCENE II

[Gothic Chamber. Slow music. St. Clare discovered, seated on sofa. Tom at left. ]

ST. CLARE:

Oh! Tom, my boy, the whole world is as empty as an egg shell.

TOM:

I know it, mas'r, I know it. But oh! if mas'r could look up — up where our dear Miss Eva is —

ST. CLARE:

Ah, Tom! I do look up; but the trouble is, I don't see anything when I do. I wish I could. It seems to be given to children and poor, honest fellows like you, to see what we cannot. How comes it?

TOM:

Thou hast hid from the wise and prudent, and revealed unto babes; even so, Father, for so it seemed good in thy sight.

ST. CLARE:

Tom, I don't believe — I've got the habit of doubting — I want to believe and I cannot.

TOM:

Dear mas'r, pray to the good Lord: "Lord, I believe; help thou my unbelief. "

ST. CLARE:

Who knows anything about anything? Was all that beautiful love and faith only one of the ever-shifting phases of human feeling, having nothing real to rest on, passing away with the little breath? And is there no more Eva — nothing?

TOM:

Oh! dear mas'r, there is. I know it; I'm sure of it. Do, do, dear mas'r, believe it!

ST. CLARE:

How do you know there is, Tom? You never saw the Lord.

TOM:

Felt Him in my soul, mas'r — feel Him now! Oh, mas'r! when I was sold away from my old woman and the children, I was jest a'most broken up — I felt as if there warn't nothing left — and then the Lord stood by me, and He says, "Fear not, Tom, " and He brings light and joy into a poor fellow's soul — makes all peace; and I's so happy, and loves everybody, and feels willin' to be jest where the Lord wants to put me. I know it couldn't come from me, 'cause I's a poor, complaining creature — it comes from above, and I know He's willin' to do for mas'r.

ST. CLARE:

[(Grasping Tom's hand. )] Tom, you love me!

TOM:

I's willin' to lay down my life this blessed day for you.

ST. CLARE:

[(Sadly. )] Poor, foolish fellow! I'm not worth the love of one good, honest heart like yours.

TOM:

Oh, mas'r! there's more than me loves you — the blessed Saviour loves you.

ST. CLARE:

How do you know that, Tom?

TOM:

The love of the Saviour passeth knowledge.

ST. CLARE:

[(Turns away. )] Singular! that the story of a man who lived and died eighteen hundred years ago can affect people so yet. But He was no man. [(Rises. )] No man ever has such long and living power. Oh! that I could believe what my mother taught me, and pray as I did when I was a boy! But, Tom, all this time I have forgotten why I sent for you. I'm going to make a freeman of you so have your trunk packed, and get ready to set out for Kentucky.

TOM:

[(Joyfully. )] Bless the Lord!

ST. CLARE:

[Dryly. )] You haven't had such very bad times here, that you need be in such a rapture, Tom.

TOM:

No, no, mas'r, 'tain't that; it's being a freeman — that's what I'm joyin' for.

ST. CLARE:

Why, Tom, don't you think, for your own part, you've been better off than to be free?

TOM:

No, indeed, Mas'r St. Clare — no, indeed!

ST. CLARE:

Why, Tom, you couldn't possibly have earned, by your work, such clothes and such living as I have given you.

TOM:

I know all that, Mas'r St. Clare — mas'r's been too good; but I'd rather have poor clothes, poor house, poor everything, and have 'em mine, than have the best, if they belong to somebody else. I had so, mas'r; I think it's natur', mas'r.

ST. CLARE:

I suppose so, Tom; and you'll be going off and leaving me in a month or so — though why you shouldn't no mortal knows.

TOM:

Not while mas'r is in trouble. I'll stay with mas'r as long as he wants me, so as I can be any use.

ST. CLARE:

[(Sadly. )] Not while I'm in trouble, Tom? And when will my trouble be over?

TOM:

When you are a believer.

ST. CLARE:

And you really mean to stay by me till that day comes? [(Smiling and laying his hand on Tom's shoulder. )] Ah, Tom! I won't keep you till that day. Go home to your wife and children, and give my love to all.

TOM:

I's faith to think that day will come — the Lord has a work for mas'r.

ST. CLARE:

A work, hey? Well, now, Tom, give me your views on what sort of a work it is — let's hear.

TOM:

Why, even a poor fellow like me has a work; and Mas'r St. Clare, that has larnin', and riches, and friends, how much he might do for the Lord.

ST. CLARE:

Tom, you seem to think the Lord needs a great deal done for him.

TOM:

We does for him when we does for his creatures.

ST. CLARE:

Good theology, Tom. Thank you, my boy; I like to hear you talk. But go now, Tom, and leave me alone. [(Exit Tom. )] That faithful fellow's words have excited a train of thoughts that almost bear me, on the strong tide of faith and feeling, to the gates of that heaven I so vividly conceive. They seem to bring me nearer to Eva.

OPHELIA:

[(Outside. )] What are you doing there, you limb of Satan? You've been stealing something, I'll be bound. [(Ophelia drags in Topsy. )]

TOPSY:

You go 'long, Miss Feely, 'tain't none o' your business.

ST. CLARE:

Heyday! what is all this commotion?

OPHELIA:

She's been stealing.

TOPSY:

[(Sobbing. )] I hain't neither.

OPHELIA:

What have you got in your bosom?

TOPSY:

I've got my hand dar.

OPHELIA:

But what have you got in your hand?

TOPSY:

Nuffin'.

OPHELIA:

That's a fib, Topsy.

TOPSY:

Well, I 'spects it is.

OPHELIA:

Give it to me, whatever it is.

TOPSY:

It's mine — I hope I may die this bressed minute, if it don't belong to me.

OPHELIA:

Topsy, I order you to give me that article; don't let me have to ask you again. [(Topsy reluctantly takes the foot of an old stocking from her bosom and hands it to Ophelia. )] Sakes alive! what is all this? [(Takes from it a lock of hair, and a small book, with a bit of crape twisted around it. )]

TOPSY:

Dat's a lock of ha'r dat Miss Eva give me — she cut if from her own beau'ful head herself.

ST. CLARE:

[(Takes book. )] Why did you wrap this [(Pointing to crape. )] around the book?

TOPSY:

'Cause — 'cause — 'cause 'twas Miss Eva's. Oh! don't take 'em away, please! [(Sits down on stage, and, putting her apron over her head, begins to sob vehemently. )]

OPHELIA:

Come, come, don't cry; you shall have them.

TOPSY:

[(Jumps up joyfully and takes them. )] I wants to keep 'em, 'cause dey makes me good; I ain't half so wicked as I used to was. [(Runs off. )]

ST. CLARE:

I really think you can make something of that girl. Any mind that is capable of a real sorrow is capable of good. You must try and do something with her.

OPHELIA:

The child has improved very much; I have great hopes of her.

ST. CLARE:

I believe I'll go down the street, a few moments, and hear the news.

OPHELIA:

Shall I call Tom to attend you?

ST. CLARE:

No, I shall be back in an hour. [(Exit. )]

OPHELIA:

He's got an excellent heart, but then he's so dreadful shiftless! [(Exit.)]

SCENE III

[Front Chamber. Enter Topsy. ]

TOPSY:

Dar's somethin' de matter wid me — I isn't a bit like myself. I haven't done anything wrong since poor Miss Eva went up in de skies and left us. When I's gwine to do anything wicked, I tinks of her, and somehow I can't do it. I's getting to be good, dat's a fact. I 'spects when I's dead I shall be turned into a little brack angel. [(Enter Ophelia. )]

OPHELIA:

Topsy, I've been looking for you; I've got something very particular to say to you.

TOPSY:

Does you want me to say the catechism?

OPHELIA:

No, not now.

TOPSY:

[(Aside. )] Golly! dat's one comfort.

OPHELIA:

Now, Topsy, I want you to try and understand what I am going to say to you.

TOPSY:

Yes, missis, I'll open my ears drefful wide.

OPHELIA:

Mr. St. Clare has given you to me, Topsy.

TOPSY:

Den I b'longs to you, don't I? Golly! I thought I always belong to you.

OPHELIA:

Not till to-day have I received any authority to call you my property.

TOPSY:

I's your property, am I? Well, if you say so, I 'spects I am.

OPHELIA:

Topsy, I can give you your liberty.

TOPSY:

My liberty?

OPHELIA:

Yes, Topsy.

TOPSY:

Has you got 'um with you?

OPHELIA:

I have, Topsy.

TOPSY:

Is it clothes or wittles?

OPHELIA:

How shiftless! Don't you know what your liberty is, Topsy?

TOPSY:

How should I know when I never seed 'um?

OPHELIA:

Topsy, I am going to leave this place; I am going many miles away — to my own home in Vermont.

TOPSY:

Den what's to become of dis chile?

OPHELIA:

If you wish to go, I will take you with me.

TOPSY:

Miss Feely, I doesn't want to leave you no how, I loves you I does.

OPHELIA:

Then you shall share my home for the rest of your days. Come, Topsy.

TOPSY:

Stop, Miss Feely; does dey hab any oberseers in Varmount?

OPHELIA:

No, Topsy.

TOPSY:

Nor cotton plantations, nor sugar factories, nor darkies, nor whipping nor nothing?

OPHELIA:

No, Topsy.

TOPSY:

By Golly! de quicker you is gwine de better den. [(Enter Tom, hastily.)]

TOM:

Oh, Miss Feely! Miss Feely!

OPHELIA:

 Gracious me, Tom! what's the matter?

TOM:

Oh, Mas'r St. Clare! Mas'r St. Clare!

OPHELIA:

 Well, Tom, well?

TOM:

They've just brought him home and I do believe he's killed?

OPHELIA:

 Killed?

TOPSY:

Oh dear! what's to become of de poor darkies now?

TOM:

He's dreadful weak. It's just as much as he can do to speak. He wanted me to call you.

OPHELIA:

 My poor cousin! Who would have thought of it? Don't say a word to his wife, Tom; the danger may not be so great as you think; it would

only distress her. Come with me; you may be able to afford some assistance. [(Exeunt. )]

## SCENE IV

[Handsome Chamber. St. Clare discovered seated on sofa. Ophelia, Tom and Topsy are clustered around him. Doctor back of sofa feeling his pulse. Scene opens to slow music. ]

ST. CLARE:

[(Raising himself feebly. )] Tom — poor fellow!

TOM:

Well, mas'r?

ST. CLARE:

I have received my death wound.

TOM:

Oh, no, no, mas'r!

ST. CLARE:

I feel that I am dying — Tom, pray!

TOM:

[(Sinking on his knees. )] I do, pray, mas'r! I do pray!

ST. CLARE:

[(After a pause. )] Tom, one thing preys upon my mind — I have forgotten to sign your freedom papers. What will become of you when I am gone?

TOM:

Don't think of that, mas'r.

ST. CLARE:

I was wrong, Tom, very wrong, to neglect it. I may be the cause of much suffering to you hereafter. Marie, my wife — she — oh! —

OPHELIA:

His mind is wandering.

ST. CLARE:

[(Energetically. )] No! it is coming home at last! (Sinks back. ) At last at last! Eva, I come! [(Dies. Music — slow curtain. )]

### END OF ACT IV

## ACT V

## SCENE I

[Enter: An Auction Mart. Uncle Tom and Emmeline at back. Adolf, Skeggs, Marks, Mann, and various spectators discovered. Marks and Mann come forward. ]

MARKS:

Hulloa, Alf! what brings you here?

MANN: Well, I was wanting a valet, and I heard that St. Clare's valet was going; I thought I'd just look at them.

MARKS:

Catch me ever buying any of St. Clare's people. Spoiled niggers every one — impudent as the devil.

MANN: Never fear that; if I get 'em, I'll soon have their airs out of them — they'll soon find that they've another kind of master to deal with than St. Clare 'Pon my word, I'll buy that fellow — I like the shape of him. [(Pointing to Adolf. )]

MARKS:

You'll find it'll take all you've got to keep him — he's deucedly extravagant.

MANN: Yes, but my lord will find that he can't be extravagant with me. Just let him be sent to the calaboose a few times, and thoroughly dressed down, I'll tell you if it don't bring him to a sense of his ways. Oh! I'll reform him, up hill and down, you'll see. I'll buy him; that's flat. [(Enter Legree, he goes up and looks at Adolf, whose boots are nicely blacked. )]

LEGREE:

A nigger with his boots blacked — bah! [(Spits on them. )] Holloa, you! [(To Tom. )] Let's see your teeth. [(Seizes Tom by the jaw and opens his mouth. )] Strip up your sleeve and show your muscle. [(Tom does so. )] Where was you rais- ed?

TOM:

In Kintuck, mas'r.

LEGREE:

What have you done?

TOM:

Had care of mas'r's farm.

LEGREE:

That's a likely story. [(Turns to Emmeline. )] You're a nice-looking girl enough. How old are you? [(Grasps her arm. )]

EMMELINE: [(Shrieking. )] Ah! you hurt me.

SKEGGS: Stop that, you minx! No whimpering here. The sale is going to begin. [(Mounts the rostrum. )] Gentlemen, the next article I shall offer you to-day is Adolf, late valet to Mr. St. Clare. How much am I offered? [(Various bids are] [made. Adolf is knocked down to Mann for eight hundred dollars. )] Gentlemen, I now offer a prime article — the quadroon girl, Emmeline, only fifteen years of age, warranted in every respect. [(Business as before. Emmeline is sold to Legree for one thousand dollars. )] Now, I shall close to-day's sale by offering you the valuable article known as Uncle Tom, the most useful nigger ever raised. Gentlemen in want of an overseer, now is the time to bid. [(Business as before. Tom is sold to Legree for twelve hundred dollars. )]

LEGREE:

Now look here, you two belong to me. [(Tom and Emmeline sink on their knees. )]

TOM:

Heaven help us, then! [(Music. Legree stands over them exulting. Picture — closed in. )]

### SCENE II

[The Garden of Miss Ophelia's House in Vermont. Enter Ophelia and Deacon Perry. ]

DEACON:

Miss Ophelia, allow me to offer you my congratulations upon your safe arrival in your native place. I hope it is your intention to pass the remainder of your days with us?

OPHELIA:

Well, Deacon, I have come here with that express purpose.

DEACON:

I presume you were not over-pleased with the South?

OPHELIA:

Well, to tell you the truth, Deacon, I wasn't; I liked the country very well, but the people there are so dreadful shiftless.

DEACON:

The result, I presume, of living in a warm climate.

OPHELIA:

Well, Deacon, what is the news among you all here?

DEACON:

Well, we live on in the same even jog-trot pace. Nothing of any conse- quence has happened — Oh! I forgot. [(Takes out handkerchief. )] I've lost my wife; my Molly has left me. [(Wipes his eyes. )]

OPHELIA:

Poor soul! I pity you, Deacon.

DEACON:

Thank you. You perceive I bear my loss with resignation.

OPHELIA:

How you must miss her tongue!

DEACON:

Molly certainly was fond of talking. She always would have the last word — heigho!

OPHELIA:

What was her complaint, Deacon?

DEACON:

A mild and soothing one, Miss Ophelia: she had a severe attack of the lockjaw.

OPHELIA:

Dreadful!

DEACON:

Wasn't it? When she found she couldn't use her tongue, she took it so much to heart that it struck to her stomach and killed her. Poor dear! Ex- cuse my handkerchief; she's been dead only eighteen months.

OPHELIA:

Why, Deacon, by this time you ought to be setting your cap for another wife.

DEACON:

Do you think so, Miss Ophelia?

OPHELIA:

I don't see why you shouldn't — you are still a good-looking man, Deacon.

DEACON:

Ah! well, I think I do wear well — in fact, I may say remarkably well. It has been observed to me before.

OPHELIA:

And you are not much over fifty?

DEACON:

Just turned of forty, I assure you.

OPHELIA:

Hale and hearty?

DEACON:

Health excellent — look at my eye! Strong as a lion — look at my arm!! A No. 1 constitution — look at my leg!!!

OPHELIA:

Have you no thoughts of choosing another partner?

DEACON:

Well, to tell you the truth, I have.

OPHELIA:

Who is she?

DEACON:

She is not far distant. [(Looks at Ophelia in an anguishing manner. )] I have her in my eye at this present moment.

OPHELIA:

[(Aside. )] Really, I believe he's going to pop. Why, surely, Deacon, you don't mean to —

DEACON:

Yes, Miss Ophelia, I do mean; and believe me, when I say — [(Looking off. )] The Lord be good to us, but I believe there is the devil coming! [(Topsy runs on, with bouquet. She is now dressed very neatly. )]

TOPSY:

Miss Feely, here is some flowers dat I hab been gathering for you. [(Gives bouquet. )]

OPHELIA:

That's a good child.

DEACON:

Miss Ophelia, who is this young person?

OPHELIA:

She is my daughter.

DEACON:

[(Aside. )] Her daughter! Then she must have married a colored man off South. I was not aware that you had been married, Miss Ophelia?

OPHELIA:

Married! Sakes alive! what made you think I had been mar- ried?

DEACON:

Good gracious, I'm getting confused. Didn't I understand you to say that this — somewhat tanned — young lady was your daughter?

OPHELIA:

Only by adoption. She is my adopted daughter.

DEACON:

O — oh! [(Aside. )] I breathe again.

TOPSY:

By Golly! dat old man's eyes stick out of 'um head dre'ful. Guess he never seed anything like me afore.

OPHELIA:

Deacon, won't you step into the house and refresh yourself after your walk?

DEACON:

I accept your polite invitation. [(Offers his arm. )] Allow me.

OPHELIA:

As gallant as ever, Deacon. I declare, you grow younger every day.

DEACON:

You can never grow old, madam.

OPHELIA:

Ah, you flatterer! [(Exeunt. )]

TOPSY:

Dar dey go, like an old goose and gander. Guess dat ole gemblemun feels kind of confectionary — rather sweet on my old missis. By Golly! she's been dre'ful kind to me ever since I come away from de South; and I loves her, I does, 'cause she takes such car' on me and gives me dese fine clothes. I tries to be good too, and I's gettin 'long 'mazin' fast. I's not so wicked as I used to was. [(Looks out. )] Holloa! dar's some one comin' here. I wonder what he wants now. [(Retires, observing. )] [Enter: (Enter Gumption Cute, very shabby, a small bundle, on a stick, over his shoulder. )]

CUTE:

By chowder, here I am again. Phew, it's a pretty considerable tall piece of walking between here and New Orleans, not to mention the wear of shoe-leather. I guess I'm about done up. If this streak of bad luck lasts much longer, I'll borrow sixpence to buy a rope, and hang myself right straight up! When I went to call on Miss Ophelia, I swow if I didn't find out that she had left for Vermont; so I kind of concluded to make tracks in that direction myself and as I didn't have any money left, why I had to foot it, and here I am in old Varmount once more. They told me Miss Ophelia lived up here. I wonder if she will remember the relationship. [(Sees Topsy. )] By chowder, there's a darkey. Look here, Charcoal!

TOPSY:

[(Comes forward. )] My name isn't Charcoal — it's Topsy.

CUTE:

Oh! your name is Topsy, is it, you juvenile specimen of Day & Martin?

TOPSY:

Tell you I don't know nothin' 'bout Day & Martin. I's Topsy and I belong to Miss Feely St.. Clare.

CUTE:

I'm much obleeged to you, you small extract of Japan, for your information. So Miss Ophelia lives up there in the white house, does she?

TOPSY:

Well, she don't do nothin' else.

CUTE:

Well, then, just locomote your pins.

TOPSY:

What — what's dat?

CUTE:

Walk your chalks!

TOPSY:

By Golly! dere ain't no chalk 'bout me.

CUTE:

Move your trotters.

TOPSY:

How you does spoke! What you mean by trotters?

CUTE:

Why, your feet, Stove Polish.

TOPSY:

What does you want me to move my feet for?

CUTE:

To tell your mistress, you ebony angel, that a gentleman wishes to see her.

TOPSY:

Does you call yourself a gentleman! By Golly! you look more like a scar'crow.

CUTE:

Now look here, you Charcoal, don't you be sassy. I'm a gentleman in distress; a done-up speculator; one that has seen better days — long time ago — and better clothes too, by chowder! My creditors are like my boots — they've no soles. I'm a victim to circumstances. I've been through much and survived it. I've taken walking exercise for the benefit of my health; but as I was trying to live on air at the same time, it was a losing speculation, 'cause it gave me such a dreadful appetite.

TOPSY:

Golly! you look as if you could eat an ox, horns and all.

CUTE:

Well, I calculate I could, if he was roasted — it's a speculation I should like to engage in. I have returned like the fellow that run away in Scripture; and if anybody's got a fatted calf they want to kill, all they got to do is to fetch him along. Do you know, Charcoal, that your mistress is a relation of mine?

TOPSY:

Is she your uncle?

CUTE:

No, no, not quite so near as that. My second cousin married her niece.

TOPSY:

And does you want to see Miss Feely?

CUTE:

I do. I have come to seek a home beneath her roof, and take care of all the spare change she don't want to use.

TOPSY:

Den just you follow me, mas'r.

CUTE:

Stop! By chowder, I've got a great idee. Say, you Day & Martin,

how should you like to enter into a speculation?

TOPSY:

Golly! I doesn't know what a spec — spec — cu — what-do-you-call-'um am.

CUTE:

Well, now, I calculate I've hit upon about the right thing. Why should I degrade the manly dignity of the Cutes by becoming a beggar — expose myself to the chance of receiving the cold shoulder as a poor relation? By chowder, my blood biles as I think of it! Topsy, you can make my fortune, and your own, too. I've an idee in my head that is worth a million of dollars.

TOPSY:

Golly! is your head worth dat? Guess you wouldn't bring dat out South for de whole of you.

CUTE:

Don't you be too severe, now, Charcoal; I'm a man of genius. Did you ever hear of Barnum?

TOPSY:

Barnum! Barnum! Does he live out South?

CUTE:

No, he lives in New York. Do you know how he made his fortin?

TOPSY:

What is him fortin, hey? Is it something he wears?

CUTE:

Chowder, how green you are!

TOPSY:

[(Indignantly. )] Sar, I hab you to know I's not green; I's brack.

CUTE:

To be sure you are, Day & Martin. I calculate, when a person says another has a fortune, he means he's got plenty of money, Charcoal.

TOPSY:

And did he make the money?

CUTE:

Sartin sure, and no mistake.

TOPSY:

Golly! now I thought money always growed.

CUTE:

Oh, git out! You are too cute — you are cuterer than I am — and I'm Cute by name and cute by nature. Well, as I was saying, Barnum made his money by exhibiting a woolly horse; now wouldn't it be an all-fired speculation to show you as the woolly gal?

TOPSY:

You want to make a sight of me?

CUTE:

I'll give you half the receipts, by chowder!

TOPSY:

Should I have to leave Miss Feely?

CUTE:

To be sure you would.

TOPSY:

Den you hab to get a woolly gal somewhere else, Mas'r Cute. [(Runs off. )]

CUTE:

There's another speculation gone to smash, by chowder! [(Exit. )]

SCENE III

[A Rude Chamber. Tom is discovered, in old clothes, seated on a stool. He holds in his hand a paper containing a curl of Eva's hair. The scene opens to the symphony of "Old Folds at Home. "]

TOM:

I have come to de dark places; I's going through de vale of shadows. My heart sinks at times and feels just like a big lump of lead. Den it gits up in my throat and chokes me till de tears roll out of my eyes; den I take out dis curl of little Miss Eva's hair, and the sight of it brings calm to my mind and I feels strong again. [(Kisses the curl and puts it in his breast — takes out a silver dollar, which is suspended around his neck by a string. )] Dere's de bright silver dollar dat Mas'r George Shelby gave me the day I was sold away from old Kentuck, and I've kept it ever since. Mas'r George must have grown to be a man by this time. I wonder if I shall ever see him again. [Enter: (Song. "Old Folks at Home. " Enter Legree, Emmeline, Sambo and Quimbo. )]

LEGREE:

Shut up, you black cuss! Did you think I wanted any of your infernal howling? [(Turns to Emmeline. )] We're home. [(Emmeline shrinks from him. He takes hold of her ear. )] You didn't ever wear earrings?

EMMELINE: [(Trembling. )] No, master.

LEGREE:

Well, I'll give you a pair, if you're a good girl. You needn't be so frightened; I don't mean to make you work very hard. You'll have fine times with me and live like a lady; only be a good girl.

EMMELINE: My soul sickens as his eyes gaze upon me. His touch makes my very flesh creep.

LEGREE:

[(Turns to Tom, and points to Sambo and Quimbo. )] Ye see what ye'd get if ye'd try to run off. These yer boys have been raised to track niggers and they'd just as soon chaw one on ye up as eat their suppers; so mind yourself. [(To Em- meline. )] Come, mistress, you go in here with me. [(Taking Emmeline's hand, and leading her off. )]

EMMELINE: [(Withdrawing her hand, and shrinking back. )] No, no! let me work in the fields; I don't want to be a lady.

LEGREE:

Oh! you're going to be contrary, are you? I'll soon take all that out of you.

EMMELINE: Kill me, if you will.

LEGREE:

Oh! you want to be killed, do you? Now come here, you Tom, you see I told you I didn't buy you jest for the common work; I mean to promote you and make a driver of you, and to-night ye may jest as well begin to get yer hand in. Now ye jest take this yer gal, and flog her; ye've seen enough on't to know how.

TOM:

I beg mas'r's pardon — hopes mas'r won't set me at that. It's what I a'nt used to — never did, and can't do — no way possible.

LEGREE:

Ye'll larn a pretty smart chance of things ye never did know before I've done with ye. [(Strikes Tom with whip, three blows. Music chord each blow. )] There! now will ye tell me ye can't do it?

TOM:

Yes, mas'r! I'm willing to work night and day, and work while there's life and breath in me; but his yer thing I can't feel it right to do, and, mas'r, I never shall do it, never!

LEGREE:

What! ye black beast! tell me ye don't think it right to do what I tell ye! What have any of you cussed cattle to do with thinking what's right? I'll put a stop to it. Why, what do ye think ye are? May be ye think yer a gentleman, master Tom, to be telling your master what's right and what a'nt! So you pre- tend it's wrong to flog the gal?

TOM:

I think so, mas'r; 'twould be downright cruel, and it's what I never will do, mas'r. If you mean to kill me, kill me; but as to raising my hand agin any one here, I never shall — I'll die first!

LEGREE:

Well, here's a pious dog at last, let down among us sinners — powerful holy critter he must be. Here, you rascal! you make believe to be so pious, didn't you never read out of your Bible, "Servants, obey your masters"? An't I your master? Didn't I pay twelve hundred dollars, cash, for all there is inside your cussed old black shell? An't you mine, body and soul?

TOM:

No, no! My soul a'nt yours, mas'r; you haven't bought it — ye can't buy it; it's been bought and paid for by one that is able to keep it, and you can't harm it!

LEGREE:

I can't? we'll see, we'll see! Here, Sambo! Quimbo! give this dog such a breaking in as he won't get over this month!

EMMELINE: Oh, no! you will not be so cruel — have some mercy! [(Clings to Tom. )]

LEGREE:

Mercy? you won't find any in this shop! Away with the black cuss! Flog him within an inch of his life! [(Music. Sambo and Quimbo seize Tom and drag him up stage. Legree seizes Em- meline, and throws her round. She falls on her knees, with her hands lifted in supplication. Legree raises his whip, as if to strike Tom. Picture closed in. )]

## SCENE IV

[Enter: Plain Chamber. Enter Ophelia, followed by Topsy. ]

OPHELIA:

A person inquiring for me, did you say, Topsy?

TOPSY:

Yes, missis.

OPHELIA:

What kind of a looking man is he?

TOPSY:

By golly! he's very queer looking man, anyway; and den he talks so dre'ful funny. What does you think? — yah! yah! he wanted to 'zibite me as de woolly gal! yah! yah!

OPHELIA:

Oh! I understand. Some cute Yankee, who wants to purchase you, to make a show of — the heartless wretch!

TOPSY:

Dat's just him, missis; dat's just his name. He tole me dat it was Cute — Mr. Cute Speculashum — dat's him.

OPHELIA:

What did you say to him, Topsy?

TOPSY:

Well, I didn't say much, it was brief and to the point — I tole him I wouldn't leave you, Miss Feely, no how.

OPHELIA:

That's right, Topsy; you know you are very comfortable here — you wouldn't fare quite so well if you went away among strangers.

TOPSY:

By golly! I know dat; you takes care on me, and makes me good. I don't steal any now, and I don't swar, and I don't dance breakdowns. Oh! I isn't so wicked as I used to was.

OPHELIA:

That's right, Topsy; now show the gentleman, or whatever he is, up.

TOPSY:

By golly! I guess he won't make much out of Miss Feely. [(Crosses and exits. )]

# Uncle Tom's Cabin

OPHELIA:

I wonder who this person can be? Perhaps it is some old acquaintance, who has heard of my arrival, and who comes on a social visit. [Enter: (Enter Cute. )]

CUTE:

Aunt, how do ye do? Well, I swan, the sight of you is good for weak eyes. [(Offers his hand. )]

OPHELIA:

[(Coldly drawing back. )] Really, sir, I can't say that I ever had the pleasure of seeing you before.

CUTE:

Well, it's a fact that you never did. You see I never happened to be in your neighborhood afore now. Of course you've heard of me? I'm one of the Cutes — Gumption Cute, the first and only son of Josiah and Maria Cute, of Oniontown, on the Onion river in the north part of this ere State of Varmount.

OPHELIA:

Can't say I ever heard the name before.

CUTE:

Well then, I calculate your memory must be a little ricketty. I'm a relation of yours.

OPHELIA:

A relation of mine! Why, I never heard of any Cutes in our fami- ly.

CUTE:

Well, I shouldn't wonder if you never did. Don't you remember your niece, Mary?

121

OPHELIA:

Of course I do. What a shiftless question!

CUTES: Well, you see my second cousin, Abijah Blake, married her. So you see that makes me a relation of yours.

OPHELIA:

Rather a distant one, I should say.

CUTE:

By chowder! I'm near enough, just at present.

OPHELIA:

Well, you certainly are a sort of connection of mine.

CUTE:

Yes, kind of sort of.

OPHELIA:

And of course you are welcome to my house, as long as you wish to make it your home.

CUTE:

By chowder! I'm booked for the next six months — this isn't a bad speculation.

OPHELIA:

I hope you left all your folks well at home?

CUTE:

Well, yes, they're pretty comfortably disposed of. Father and mother's dead, and Uncle Josh has gone to California. I am the only represen- tative of the Cutes left.

OPHELIA:

There doesn't seem to be a great deal of you left. I declare, you are positively in rags.

CUTE:

Well, you see, the fact is, I've been speculating — trying to get bank-notes — specie-rags, as they say — but I calculate I've turned out rags of another sort.

OPHELIA:

I'm sorry for your ill luck, but I am afraid you have been shiftless.

CUTE:

By chowder! I've done all that a fellow could do. You see, somehow, everything I take hold of kind of bursts up.

OPHELIA:

Well, well, perhaps you'll do better for the future; make yourself at home. I have got to see to some house-hold matters, so excuse me for a short time. [(Aside. )] Impudent and shiftless. [(Exit. )]

CUTE:

By chowder! I rather guess that this speculation will hitch. She's a good-natured old critter; I reckon I'll be a son to her while she lives, and take care of her valuables arter she's a defunct departed. I wonder if they keep the vittles in this ere room? Guess not. I've got extensive accommodations for all sorts of eatables. I'm a regular vacuum, throughout — pockets and all. I'm chuck full of emptiness. [(Looks out. )] Holloa! who's this elderly individual coming up stairs? He looks like a compound essence of starch and dignity. I wonder if he isn't another relation of mine. I should like a rich old fellow now for an uncle. [Enter: (Enter Deacon Perry. )]

DEACON:

Ha! a stranger here!

CUTE:

How d'ye do?

DEACON:

You are a friend to Miss Ophelia, I presume?

CUTE:

Well, I rather calculate that I am a leetle more than a friend.

DEACON:

[(Aside. )] Bless me! what can he mean by those mysterious words? Can he be her — no I don't think he can. She said she wasn't — well, at all events, it's very suspicious.

CUTE:

The old fellow seems kind of stuck up.

DEACON:

You are a particular friend to Miss Ophelia, you say?

CUTE:

Well, I calculate I am.

DEACON:

Bound to her by any tender tie?

CUTE:

It's something more than a tie — it's a regular double-twisted knot.

DEACON:

Ah! just as I suspected. [(Aside. )] Might I inquire the nature of that tie?

CUTE:

Well, it's the natural tie of relationship.

DEACON:

A relation — what relation?

CUTE:

Why, you see, my second cousin, Abijah Blake, married her niece, Mary.

DEACON:

Oh! is that all?

CUTE:

By chowder, ain't that enough?

DEACON:

Then you are not her husband?

CUTE:

To be sure I ain't. What put that ere idee into your cranium?

DEACON:

[(Shaking him vigorously by the hand. )] My dear sir, I'm delighted to see you.

CUTE:

Holloa! you ain't going slightly insane, are you?

DEACON:

No, no fear of that; I'm only happy, that's all.

CUTE:

I wonder if he's been taking a nipper?

DEACON:

As you are a relation of Miss Ophelia's, I think it proper that I should make you my confidant; in fact, let you into a little scheme that I have lately conceived.

CUTE:

Is it a speculation?

DEACON:

Well, it is, just at present; but I trust before many hours to make it a surety.

CUTE:

By chowder! I hope it won't serve you the way my speculations have served me. But fire away, old boy, and give us the prospectus.

DEACON:

Well, then, my young friend, I have been thinking, ever since Miss Ophelia returned to Vermont, that she was just the person to fill the place of my lamented Molly.

CUTE:

Say, you, you couldn't tell us who your lamented Molly was, could you?

DEACON:

Why, the late Mrs. Perry, to be sure.

CUTE:

Oh! then the lamented Molly was your wife?

DEACON:

She was.

CUTE:

And now you wish to marry Miss Ophelia?

DEACON:

Exactly.

CUTE:

[(Aside. )] Consarn this old porpoise! if I let him do that he'll Jew me out of my living. By chowder! I'll put a spoke in his wheel.

DEACON:

Well, what do you say? will you intercede for me with your aunt?

CUTE:

No! bust me up if I do!

DEACON:

No?

CUTE:

No, I tell you. I forbid the bans. Now, ain't you a purty individual, to talk about getting married, you old superannuated Methuselah specimen of humanity! Why, you've got one foot in etarnity already, and t'other ain't fit to stand on. Go home and go to bed! have your head shaved, and send for a lawyer to make your will, leave your property to your heirs — if you hain't got any, why leave it to me — I'll take care of it, and charge nothing for the trouble.

DEACON:

Really, sir, this language to one of my standing, is highly in-decorous — it's more, sir, than I feel willing to endure, sir. I shall expect an ex- planation, sir.

CUTE:

Now, you see, old gouty toes, you're losing your temper.

DEACON:

Sir, I'm a deacon; I never lost my temper in all my life, sir.

CUTE:

Now, you see, you're getting excited; you had better go; we can't have a disturbance here!

DEACON:

No, sir! I shall not go, sir! I shall not go until I have seen Miss Ophelia. I wish to know if she will countenance this insult.

CUTE:

Now keep cool, old stick-in-the-mud! Draw it mild, old timber-toes!

DEACON:

Damn it all, sir, what —

CUTE:

Oh! only think, now, what would people say to hear a deacon swearing like a trooper?

DEACON:

Sir — I — you — this is too much, sir.

CUTE:

Well, now, I calculate that's just about my opinion, so we'll have no more of it. Get out of this! start your boots, or by chowder! I'll pitch you from one end of the stairs to the other. [Enter: (Enter Ophelia)]

OPHELIA:

Hoity toity! What's the meaning of all these loud words?

CUTE:

[(Together. )] Well, you see, Aunt —

DEACON:

Miss Ophelia, I beg —

CUTE:

Now, look here, you just hush your yap! How can I fix up matters if you keep jabbering?

OPHELIA:

Silence! for shame, Mr. Cute. Is that the way you speak to the deacon?

CUTE:

Darn the deacon!

OPHELIA:

Deacon Perry, what is all this?

DEACON:

Madam, a few words will explain everything. Hearing from this person that he was your nephew, I ventured to tell him that I cherished hopes of making you my wife, where upon he flew into a violent passion, and ordered me out of the house.

OPHELIA:

Does this house belong to you or me, Mr. Cute?

CUTE:

Well, to you, I reckon.

OPHELIA:

Then how dare you give orders in it?

CUTE:

Well, I calculated that you wouldn't care about marrying old half a century there.

OPHELIA:

That's enough; I will marry him; and as for you, [(Points. )] get out.

CUTE:

Get out?

OPHELIA:

 Yes; the sooner the better.

CUTE:

Darned if I don't serve him out first though. [(Music. Cute makes a dash at Deacon, who gets behind Ophelia. Topsy enters, with a broom and beats Cute around stage. Ophelia faints in Deacon's arms. Cute falls, and Topsy butts him kneeling over him. Quick drop. )]

## ACT VI

## SCENE I

[Dark landscape. An old, roofless shed. Tom is discovered in shed, lying on some old cotton bagging. Cassy kneels by his side, holding a cup to his lips. ]

CASSY:

Drink all ye want. I knew how it would be. It isn't the first time I've been out in the night, carrying water to such as you.

TOM:

[(Returning cup. )] Thank you, missis.

CASSY:

Don't call me missis. I'm a miserable slave like yourself — a lower one than you can ever be! It's no use, my poor fellow, this you've been trying to do. You were a brave fellow. You had the right on your side; but it's all in vain for you to struggle. You are in the Devil's hands; he is the strongest, and you must give up.

TOM:

Oh! how can I give up?

CASSY:

You see you don't know anything about it; I do. Here you are, on a lone plantation, ten miles from any other, in the swamps; not a white person here who could testify, if you were burned alive. There's no law here that can do you, or any of us, the least good; and this man! there's no earthly thing that he is not bad enough to do. I could make one's hair rise, and their teeth chatter, if I should only tell what I've seen and been knowing to here; and it's no use resisting! Did I want to live with him? Wasn't I a woman delicately bred? and he! — Father in Heaven! what was he and is he? And yet I've lived with him these five years, and cursed every moment of my life, night and day.

TOM:

Oh heaven! have you quite forgot us poor critters?

CASSY:

And what are these miserable low dogs you work with, that you should suffer on their account? Every one of them would turn against you the first time they get a chance. They are all of them as low and cruel to each other as they can be; there's no use in your suffering to keep from hurting them?

TOM:

What made 'em cruel? If I give out I shall get used to it and grow, little by little, just like 'em. No, no, Missis, I've lost everything, wife, and children, and home, and a kind master, and he would have set me free if he'd only lived a day longer — I've lost everything in this world, and now I can't lose heaven, too: no I can't get to be wicked besides all.

CASSY:

But it can't be that He will lay sin to our account; he won't charge it to us when we are forced to it; he'll charge it to them that drove us to it. Can I do anything more for you? Shall I give you some more water?

TOM:

Oh missis! I wish you'd go to Him who can give you living waters!

CASSY:

Go to him! Where is he? Who is he?

TOM:

Our Heavenly Father!

CASSY:

 I used to see the picture of him, over the altar, when I was a girl but he isn't here! there's nothing here but sin, and long, long despair! There, there, don't talk any more, my poor fellow. Try to sleep, if you can. I must hasten back, lest my absence be noted. Think of me when I am gone, Uncle Tom, and pray, pray for me. [(Music. Exit Cassy. Tom sinks back to sleep. )]

## SCENE II

[Street in New Orleans. Enter George Shelby. ]

GEORGE:

At length my mission of mercy is nearly finished, I have reached my journey's end. I have now but to find the house of Mr. St. Clare, re-purchase old Uncle Tom, and convey him back to his wife and children, in old Kentucky. Some one approaches; he may, perhaps, be able to give me the information I re- quire. I will accost him. [(Enter Marks. )] Pray, sir, can you tell me where Mr. St. Clare dwells?

MARKS:

Where I don't hink you'll be in a hurry to seek him.

GEORGE:

And where is that?

MARKS:

In the grave!

GEORGE:

Stay, sir! you may be able to give me some information concern- ing Mr. St. Clare.

MARKS:

I beg pardon, sir, I am a lawyer; I can't afford to give anything

GEORGE:

But you would have no objections to selling it?

MARKS:

Not the slightest.

GEORGE:

What do you value it at?

MARKS:

Well, say five dollars, that's reasonable.

GEORGE:

There they are. [(Gives money. )] Now answer me to the best of your ability. Has the death of St. Clare caused his slaves to be sold?

MARKS:

It has.

GEORGE:

How were they sold?

MARKS:

At auction — they went dirt cheap.

GEORGE:

How were they bought — all in one lot?

MARKS:

No, they went to different bidders.

GEORGE:

Was you present at the sale?

MARKS:

I was.

GEORGE:

Do you remember seeing a negro among them called Tom?

MARKS:

What, Uncle Tom?

GEORGE:

The same — who bought him?

MARKS:

A Mr. Legree.

GEORGE:

Where is his plantation?

MARKS:

Up in Louisiana, on the Red River; but a man never could find it, unless he had been there before.

GEORGE:

Who could I get to direct me there?

MARKS:

Well, stranger, I don't know of any one just at present 'cept myself, could find it for you; it's such an out-of-the-way sort of hole; and if you are a mind to come down handsomely, why, I'll do it.

GEORGE:

The reward shall be ample.

MARKS:

Enough said, stranger; let's take the steamboat at once. [(Exeunt. )]

### SCENE III

[A Rough Chamber. Enter Legree. Sits. ]

LEGREE:

Plague on that Sambo, to kick up this yer row between Tom and the new hands. [(Cassy steals on and stands behind him. )] The fellow won't be fit to work for a week now, right in the press of the season.

CASSY:

Yes, just like you.

LEGREE:

Hah! you she-devil! you've come back, have you? [(Rises)]

CASSY:

Yes, I have; come to have my own way, too.

LEGREE:

You lie, you jade! I'll be up to my word. Either behave yourself or stay down in the quarters and fare and work with the rest.

CASSY:

I'd rather, ten thousand times, live in the dirtiest hole at the quarters, than be under your hoof!

LEGREE:

But you are under my hoof, for all that, that's one comfort; so sit down here and listen to reason. [(Grasps her wrist. )]

CASSY:

Simon Legree, take care! [(Legree lets go his hold. )] You're afraid of me, Simon, and you've reason to be; for I've got the Devil in me!

LEGREE:

I believe to my soul you have. After all, Cassy, why can't you be friends with me, as you used to?

CASSY:

[(Bitterly. )] Used to!

LEGREE:

I wish, Cassy, you'd behave yourself decently.

CASSY:

You talk about behaving decently! and what have you been doing? You haven't even sense enough to keep from spoiling one of your best hands, right in the most pressing season, just for your devilish temper.

LEGREE:

I was a fool, it's fact, to let any such brangle come up. Now when Tom set up his will he had to be broke in.

CASSY:

You'll never break him in.

LEGREE:

Won't I? I'd like to know if I won't? He'd be the first nigger that ever come it round me! I'll break every bone in his body but he shall give up. [(Enter Sambo, with a paper in his hand, stands bowing. )] What's that, you dog?

SAMBO:

It's a witch thing, mas'r.

LEGREE:

A what?

SAMBO:

Something that niggers gits from witches. Keep 'em from feeling when they's flogged. He had it tied round his neck with a black string. [(Legree takes the paper and opens it. A silver dollar drops on the stage, and a long curl of light hair twines around his finger. )]

LEGREE:

Damnation. [(Stamping and writhing, as if the hair burned him. )] Where did this come from? Take it off! burn it up! [(Throws the curl away. )]

What did you bring it to me for?

SAMBO:

[(Trembling. )] I beg pardon, mas'r; I thought you would like to see um.

LEGREE:

Don't you bring me any more of your devilish things. [(Shakes his fist at Sambo who runs off. Legree kicks the dollar after him. )] Blast it! where did he get that? If it didn't look just like — whoo! I thought I'd forgot that. Curse me if I think there's any such thing as forgetting anything, any how.

CASSY:

What is the matter with you, Legree? What is there in a simple curl of fair hair to appall a man like you — you who are familiar with every form of cruetly.

LEGREE:

Cassy, to-night the past has been recalled to me — the past that I have so long and vainly striven to forget.

CASSY:

Has aught on this earth power to move a soul like thine?

LEGREE:

Yes, for hard and reprobate as I now seem, there has been a time when I have been rocked on the bosom of a mother, cradled with prayers and pious hymns, my now seared brow bedewed with the waters of holy baptism.

CASSY:

[(Aside. )] What sweet memories of childhood can thus soften down that heart of iron?

LEGREE:

In early childhood a fair-haired woman has led me, at the sound of Sabbath bells, to worship and to pray. Born of a hard-tempered sire, on whom that gentle woman had wasted a world of unvalued love, I followed in the steps of my fgather. Boisterous, unruly and tyrannical, I despised all her counsel, and would have none of her reproof, and, at an early age, broke from her to seek my fortunes on the sea. I never came home but once after that; and then my mother, with the yearning of a heart that must love something, and had nothing else to love, clung to me, and sought with passionate prayers and entreaties to win me from a life of sin.

CASSY:

That was your day of grace, Legree; then good angels called you, and mercy held you by the hand.

LEGREE:

My heart inly relented; there was a conflict, but sin got the victory, and I set all the force of my rough nature against the conviction of my cons- cience. I drank and swore, was wilder and more brutal than ever. And one night, when my mother, in the last agony of her despair, knelt at my feet, I spurned her from me, threw her senseless on the floor, and with brutal curses fl- ed to my ship.

CASSY:

Then the fiend took thee for his own.

LEGREE:

The next I heard of my mother was one night while I was carous- ing among drunken companions. A letter was put in my hands. I opened it, and a lock of long, curling hair fell from it, and twined about my fingers, even as that lock twined but now. The letter told me that my mother was dead, and that dying she blest and forgave me! [(Buries his face in his hands. )]

CASSY:

Why did you not even then renounce your evil ways?

LEGREE:

There is a dread, unhallowed necromancy of evil, that turns things sweetest and holiest to phantoms of horror and afright. That pale, loving mother, — her dying prayers, her forgiving love, — wrought in my demoniac heart of sin only as a damning sentence, bringing with it a fearful looking for of judgment and fiery indignation.

CASSY:

And yet you would not strive to avert the doom that threatened you.

LEGREE:

I burned the lock of hair and I burned the letter; and when I saw them hissing and crackling in the flame, inly shuddered as I thought of everlasting fires! I tried to drink and revel, and swear away the memory; but often in the deep night, whose solemn stillness arraings the soul in forced com- munion with itself, I have seen that pale mother rising by my bed-side, and felt the soft twining of that hair around my fingers, 'till the cold sweat would roll down my face, and I would spring from my bed in horror — horror! [(Falls in] [chair — After a pause. )] What the devil ails me? Large drops of sweat stand on my forehead, and my heart beats heavy and thick with fear. I thought I saw something white rising and glimmering in the gloom before me, and it seemed to bear my mother's face! I know one thing; I'll let that fellow Tom alone, after this. What did I want with his cussed paper? I believe I am bewitched sure enough! I've been shivering and sweating ever since! Where did he get that hair? It couldn't have been that! I burn'd that up, I know I did! It would be a joke if hair could rise from the dead! I'll have Sambo and Quimbo up here to sing and dance one of their dances, and keep off these horrid notions. Here, Sambo! Quimbo! [(Exit. )]

CASSY:

Yes, Legree, that golden tress was charmed; each hair had in it a spell of terror and remorse for thee, and was used by a mightier power to bind thy cruel hands from inflicting uttermost evil on the helpless! [(Exit. )]

SCENE IV

[Street. Enter Marks meeting Cute, who enters dressed in an old faded uniform]

MARKS:

By the land, stranger, but it strikes me that I've seen you somewhere before.

CUTE:

By chowder! do you know now, that's just what I was a going to say?

MARKS:

Isn't your name Cute?

CUTE:

You're right, I calculate. Yours is Marks, I reckon.

MARKS:

Just so.

CUTE:

Well, I swow, I'm glad to see you. [(They shake hands. )] How's your wholesome?

MARKS:

Hearty as ever. Well, who would have thought of ever seeing you again. Why, I thought you was in Vermont?

CUTE:

Well, so I was. You see I went there after that rich relation of mine — but the speculation didn't turn out well.

MARKS:

How so?

CUTE:

Why, you see, she took a shine to an old fellow — Deacon Abraham Perry — and married him.

MARKS:

Oh, that rather put your nose out of joint in that quarter.

CUTE:

Busted me right up, I tell you. The Deacon did the hand-some thing though, he said if I would leave the neighborhood and go out South again, he'd stand the damage. I calculate I didn't give him much time to change his mind. and so, you see, here I am again.

MARKS:

What are you doing in that soldier rig?

CUTE:

Oh, this is my sign.

MARKS:

Your sign?

CUTE:

Yes; you see, I'm engaged just at present in an all-fired good speculation, I'm a Fillibusterow.

MARKS:

A what?

CUTE:

A Fillubusterow! Don't you know what that is? It's Spanish for Cuban Volunteer; and means a chap that goes the whole perker for glory and all that ere sort of thing.

MARKS:

Oh! you've joined the order of the Lone Star!

CUTE:

You've hit it. You see I bought this uniform at a second hand clothing store, I puts it on and goes to a benevolent individual and I says to him, — appealing to his feelings, — I'm one of the fellows that went to Cuba and got massacred by the bloody Spaniards. I'm in a destitute condition — give me a trifle to pay my passage back, so I can whop the tyrannical cusses and avenge my brave fellow soger what got slewed there.

MARKS:

How pathetic!

CUTE:

I tell you it works up the feelings of benevolent individuals dreadful-ly. It draws tears from their eyes and money from their pockets. By chowder! one old chap gave me a hundred dollars to help on the cause.

MARKS:

I admire a genius like yours.

CUTE:

But I say, what are you up to?

MARKS:

I am the traveling companion of a young gentleman by the name of Shelby, who is going to the plantation of a Mr. Legree of the Red River, to buy an old darkey who used to belong to his father.

CUTE:

Legree — Legree? Well, now, I calculate I've heard that ere name afore.

MARKS:

Do you remember that man who drew a bowie knife on you in New Orleans?

CUTE:

By chowder! I remember the circumstance just as well as if it was yesterday; but I can't say that I recollect much about the man, for you see I was in something of a hurry about that time and didn't stop to take a good look at him.

MARKS:

Well, that man was this same Mr. Legree.

CUTE:

Do you know, now, I should like to pay that critter off!

MARKS:

Then I'll give you an opportunity.

CUTE:

Chowder! how will you do that?

MARKS:

Do you remember the gentleman that interfered between you and Legree?

CUTE:

Yes — well?

MARKS:

He received the blow that was intended for you, and died from the effects of it. So, you see, Legree is a murderer, and we are only witnesses of the deed. His life is in our hands.

CUTE:

Let's have him right up and make him dance on nothing to the tune of Yandee Doodle!

MARKS:

Stop a bit. Don't you see a chance for a profitable speculation?

CUTE:

A speculation! Fire away, don't be bashful, I'm the man for a speculation.

MARKS:

I have made a deposition to the Governor of the state on all the particulars of that affair at Orleans.

CUTE:

What did you do that for?

MARKS:

To get a warrant for his arrest.

CUTE:

Oh! and have you got it?

MARKS:

Yes; here it is. [(Takes out paper. )]

CUTE:

Well, now, I don't see how you are going to make anything by that bit of paper?

MARKS:

But I do. I shall say to Legree, I have got a warrant against you for murder; my friend, Mr. Cute, and myself are the only witnesses who can ap- pear against you. Give us a thousand dollars, and we will tear the warrant and be silent.

CUTE:

Then Mr. Legree forks over a thousand dollars, and your friend Cute pockets five hundred of it, is that the calculation?

MARKS:

If you will join me in the undertaking.

CUTE:

I'll do it, by chowder!

MARKS:

Your hand to bind the bargain.

CUTE:

I'll stick by you thro' thick and thin.

MARKS:

Enough said.

CUTE:

Then shake. [(They shake hands. )]

MARKS:

But I say, Cute, he may be contrary and show fight.

CUTE:

Never mind, we've got the law on our side, and we're bound to stir him up. If he don't come down handsomely we'll present him with a neck-tie made of hemp!

MARKS:

I declare you're getting spunky.

CUTE:

Well, I reckon, I am. Let's go and have something to drink. Tell you what, Marks, if we don't get him, we'll have his hide, by chowder! [(Exeunt, arm in arm. )]

SCENE V

[Rough Chamber. Enter Legree, followed by Sambo. ]

LEGREE:

Go and send Cassy to me.

SAMBO:

Yes, mas'r. [(Exit. )]

LEGREE:

Curse the woman! she's got a temper worse than the devil; I shall do her an injury one of these days, if she isn't careful. [(Re-enter Sambo, frightened. )] What's the matter with you, you black scoundrel?

SAMBO:

S'help me, mas'r, she isn't dere.

LEGREE:

I suppose she's about the house somewhere?

SAMBO:

No, she isn't, mas'r; I's been all over de house and I can't find nothing of her nor Emmeline.

LEGREE:

Bolted, by the Lord! Call out the dogs! saddle my horse. Stop! are you sure they really have gone?

SAMBO:

Yes, mas'r; I's been in every room 'cept the haunted garret and dey wouldn't go dere.

LEGREE:

I have it! Now, Sambo, you jest go and walk that Tom up here, right away! [(Exit Sambo. )] The old cuss is at the bottom of this yer whole matter; and I'll have it out of his infernal black hide, or I'll know the reason why! I hate him — I hate him! And isn't he mine? Can't I do what I like with him? Who's to hinder, I wonder? [(Tom is dragged on by Sambo and Quimbo, Legree grimly confronting Tom. )] Well, Tom, do you know I've made up my mind to kill you?

TOM:

It's very likely, Mas'r.

LEGREE:

I — have — done — just — that — thing, Tom, unless you'll tell me what do you know about these yer gals? [(Tom is silent. )] D'ye hear? Speak!

TOM:

I han't got anything to tell, mas'r.

LEGREE:

Do you dare to tell me, you old black rascal, you don't know? Speak! Do you know anything?

TOM:

I know, mas'r; but I can't tell anything. I can die!

LEGREE:

Hark ye, Tom! ye think, 'cause I have let you off before, I don't mean what I say; but, this time, I have made up my mind, and counted the cost. You've always stood it out agin me; now, I'll conquer ye or kill ye! one or t'other. I'll count every drop of blood there is in you, and take 'em, one by one, 'till ye give up!

TOM:

Mas'r, if you was sick, or in trouble, or dying, and I could save you, I'd give you my heart's blood; and, if taking every drop of blood in this poor old body would save your precious soul, I'd give 'em freely. Do the worst you can, my troubles will be over soon; but if

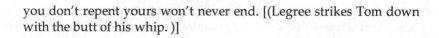

you don't repent yours won't never end. [(Legree strikes Tom down with the butt of his whip. )]

LEGREE:

How do you like that?

SAMBO:

He's most gone, mas'r!

TOM:

[(Rises feebly on his hands. )] There an't no more you can do. I forgive you with all my soul. [(Sinks back, and is carried off by Sambo and Quimbo. )]

LEGREE:

I believe he's done for finally. Well, his mouth is shut up at last — that's one comfort. [(Enter George Shelby, Marks and Cute. )] Strangers! Well what do you want?

GEORGE:

I understand that you bought in New Orleans a negro named Tom?

LEGREE:

Yes, I did buy such a fellow, and a devil of a bargain I had of it, too! I believe he's trying to die, but I don't know as he'll make it out.

GEORGE:

Where is he? Let me see him?

SAMBO:

Dere he is. [(Points to Tom). ]

LEGREE:

How dare you speak? [(Drives Sambo and Quimbo off. George exits.)]

CUTE:

Now's the time to nab him.

MARKS:

How are you, Mr. Legree?

LEGREE:

What the devil brought you here?

MARKS:

This little bit of paper. I arrest you for the murder of Mr. St. Clare. What do you say to that?

LEGREE:

This is my answer! [(Makes a blow at Marks, who dodges, and Cute receives the blow — he cries out and runs off, Marks fires at Legree, and follows Cute. )] I am hit! — the game's up! [(Falls dead. Quimbo and Sambo return and carry him off laughing. )] [Enter: (George Shelby enters, supporting Tom. Music. They advance to front and Tom falls. )]

GEORGE:

Oh! dear Uncle Tom! do wake — do speak once more! look up! Here's Master George — your own little Master George. Don't you know me?

TOM:

[(Opening his eyes and speaking in a feeble tone. )] Mas'r George! Bless de Lord! it's all I wanted! They hav'n't forgot me! It warms my soul; it does my old heart good! Now I shall die content!

GEORGE:

You shan't die! you mustn't die, nor think of it. I have come to buy you, and take you home.

TOM:

Oh, Mas'r George, you're too late. The Lord has bought me, and is going to take me home.

GEORGE:

Oh! don't die. It will kill me — it will break my heart to think what you have suffered, poor, poor fellow!

TOM:

Don't call me, poor fellow! I have been poor fellow; but that's all past and gone now. I'm right in the door, going into glory! Oh, Mas'r George! Heaven has come! I've got the victory, the Lord has given it to me! Glory be to His name! [(Dies. )] [(Solemn music. George covers Uncle Tom with his cloak, and kneels over him. Clouds work on and conceal them, and then work off. )]

SCENE VII

[Gorgeous clouds, tinted with sunlight. Eva, robed in white, is discovered on the back of a milk-white dove, with expanded wings, as if just soaring upward. Her hands are extended in benediction over St. Clare and Uncle Tom who are kneeling and gazing up to her. Expressive music. Slow curtain. ]

END